THE MOTHER CHURCH

THE MOTHER CHURCH

A Church Leader's Guide to Birthing and Nurturing Thriving New Congregations

JOHN C. BANGS

iUniverse, Inc.
New York Bloomington

The Mother Church
A Church Leader's Guide to Birthing and Nurturing Thriving
New Congregations

iUniverse books may be ordered through booksellers or by contacting:

iUniverse
1663 Liberty Drive
Bloomington, IN 47403
www.iuniverse.com
1-800-Authors (1-800-288-4677)

ISBN: 978-1-4502-2100-9 (sc)
ISBN: 978-1-4502-2101-6 (ebook)
ISBN: 978-1-4502-2099-6 (dj)

Printed in the United States of America

iUniverse rev. date: 7/15/2010

*All scripture is taken from the Holy Bible, Today's New
International Version™ (TNIV®) Copyright 2001, 2005 by
International Bible Society®. All rights reserved worldwide.*

To the members of Hillside Chapel and to her two parent churches: Eastside Foursquare Church and Westminster Chapel

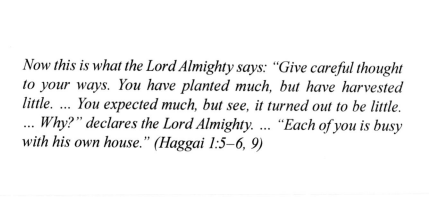

Now this is what the Lord Almighty says: "Give careful thought to your ways. You have planted much, but have harvested little. ... You expected much, but see, it turned out to be little. ... Why?" declares the Lord Almighty. ... "Each of you is busy with his own house." (Haggai 1:5–6, 9)

ACKNOWLEDGMENTS

This work is based upon research and publications by exemplary leaders in the church-multiplication movement as it is practiced in North America and worldwide. These individuals have changed the world and advanced the cause of Christ in a manner unparalleled in our time. I am exceptionally thankful to my colleagues at Northwest University and at Fuller Seminary Northwest who have provided friendship, guidance, assistance, and space in an otherwise full schedule.

My ultimate and unmitigated thanks, appreciation, and love go to my wife Treesa and to my eight children, Leah, Britton, Natalie, Taban, Kape, Latio, Kaku, and Mariam, who have been incredibly supportive and have extended nothing but encouragement as I have dedicated much time to this project. You are my life. Finally, I thank God through Jesus Christ for an abundant life filled with rich blessings and for the hope of an eternity filled with God's immediate presence. "To them God has chosen to make known … the glorious riches of this mystery, which is Christ in you, the hope of glory" (Colossians 1:27).

CONTENTS

INTRODUCTION

In 1990, C. Peter Wagner released his catalytic book, *Church Planting for a Greater Harvest*. Wagner effectively launched the modern church planting movement with his now-famous proclamation that "the single most effective evangelistic methodology under heaven is planting new churches."[1] Since then, many thousands of new congregations have been launched, with pioneer pastors clutching the Bible in one hand and Wagner's book in the other. Thank God for this movement! It would be reasonable to estimate that multiple hundreds of thousands of people have become followers of Jesus Christ as a result of the modern church-planting movement.

One characteristic of the literature of this movement has been an almost singular focus on the individual who is sent out to lead the new congregation, rather than on the vital role of the sending or sponsoring church. Practically all the books are written with one target in mind: this individual leader, the pioneer pastor, usually referred to as the "church planter." Another characteristic has been the tacit acceptance of an agricultural metaphor—church planting—rather than a biological one—mothering or parenting. For this reason, this book is not written for pioneer pastors; it is written for the

1   C. Peter Wagner, *Church Planting for a Greater Harvest: A Comprehensive Guide* (Ventura, CA: Regal, 1990), 11.

leaders of potential mother churches. If you are an aspiring pioneer pastor, you are, of course, free to read on. I hope you will. But please also give copies of this book to the pastors, elders, deacons, and council members of your mother church. Your experience will be significantly enhanced if you do. If you are a pastor or lay leader of a potential mother church, this book is for you. Please read on with care. The book is designed to help you assess whether and when the birthing of a new church is a good idea for your congregation and to provide you with tools to birth and nurture healthy, thriving, life-giving new churches.

With this book, I hope to accomplish something similar to what Wagner accomplished: I want to spark a movement. Building on Wagner's famous statement, I propose that the single most effective church-*multiplication* methodology under heaven is *parenting* new churches.[2] I believe that this powerful movement must be recast under a parenting metaphor for two reasons.

First, though the movement as a whole has been tremendously fruitful, the majority of individual works have failed to thrive. This has resulted in unacceptably high costs in terms of leadership burnout and congregational discouragement. At a fundamental level, parenting is a more nurturing metaphor than planting, and new congregations need more nurturance than they have historically received.

Second, though the church planting movement has resulted in the establishment of thousands of new congregations, we need more. New churches are the most powerful means to reach emerging generations with the gospel, and the North American church is behind in this task. The parenting metaphor transfers responsibility for the establishment of new churches <u>from the denom</u>ination to the congregation, effectively creating

2   Edward J. Stetzer, *Planting New Churches in a Postmodern Age* (Nashville, TN: Broadman & Holman, 2003), 76. "The best church planting occurs when a sponsor/mother church is actively involved in the planting of new churches."

hundreds of thousands more potential parents. If we need more children—more brand-new, healthy baby churches—we need more parents.

I hope this book will be a catalyst for two major readjustments in North American new church development, both of which are implied in the parent-church metaphor:

1. That genuine parental nurture will be invested in every new church project, resulting in healthy, thriving congregations and leaders.
2. That every church will see the parenting of baby churches as a normal, expected, and natural part of its congregational life cycle.

Though the evangelistic effectiveness of new congregations among emerging generations is widely known, the progress of the gospel and church attendance among young adults is in steady decline. We are not starting enough new churches, and most of those we start do not thrive.

The single most important *congregational* priority under heaven must be reaching *emerging generations.*[3] The single most effective *emerging-generation-reaching* methodology under heaven is parenting new churches. The single most costly *evangelistic mistake* congregations can make is the *failure to reproduce themselves* in new congregations for emerging generations. It could even be said that, if a majority of individual congregations in North America fail to rise to the significant challenge of parenting new churches, we could witness a dramatic reduction in the vitality, relevance, and

---

3   George Barna, "Most Twentysomethings Put Christianity on the Shelf Following Spiritually Active Teen Years," http://www.barna.org/barna-update/article/16-teensnext-gen/147-most-twentysomethings-put-christianity-on-the-shelf-following-spiritually-active-teen-years (accessed March 19, 2010). "61% of today's young adults ... had been churched at one point during their teen years but they are now spiritually disengaged."

impact of the Christian faith for North America's emerging generations.[4]

My chief goal in this work is to encourage pastors, elders, and other agenda-setting leaders of existing North American churches to consider seriously whether their churches might be (1) ready, and (2) called by God to parent new congregations. Not all will answer in the affirmative, but many will. I want to spur these leaders to *take action* in regard to church-multiplication and to take the right kind of action: investing the resources of the congregations they lead in planning, birthing, and nurturing intentional new congregations for new generations.

If you are one of these leaders, please prayerfully consider your congregation's next steps as you engage the pages that follow.

---

4   Darrell L. Guder and Lois Barrett, *Missional Church: A Vision for the Sending of the Church in North America*, The Gospel and Our Culture Series (Grand Rapids, MI: William B. Eerdmans, 1998), 59. Commenting on the secularization of Canada, Guder writes, "Whereas 50–60 percent of Protestant members had been active in weekly attendance up to that time, participation rates dropped by almost two-thirds within twenty years. The decline of Catholic participation in Quebec was even more pronounced … It dropped from 80 percent to under 40 percent during the same twenty-year period. In the throes of this upheaval, many pastors and churches concentrated on maintaining the faith of their active members, and because of this focus, a whole generation of youth and young adults was lost to the church."

PART ONE:

WHY

Chapter 1
Church Parenting: A Better Metaphor

We do not think good metaphors are anything very important, but I think a good metaphor is something even the police should keep an eye on.[5]
—*Georg Christoph Lichtenberg*

What if every married couple in North America chose to forego having children in order to give themselves more fully to the accomplishment of personal and career goals? What if going childless were the rule instead of the exception? Several obvious results would seem positive.

Businesses would be more productive. Consider what could be done with twice the workforce, the ability to work almost interminable hours, undistracted devotion to business objectives, evenings spent networking at parties and dinners, and more time for education. The population would likely be healthier. Imagine the energy and fitness we could achieve

---

5 Leonard I. Sweet, "A New Reformation: Re-Creating Worship for a Postmodern World," in *Worship at the Next Level*, ed. Tim A. Dearborn (Grand Rapids, MI: Baker, 2004), 108. Sweet attributes the quote to Philosopher Friedrich Nietzsche, who was an admirer of Lichtenberg.

with excess time to spend with physical trainers, masseuses, spiritual directors, and psychologists. Individuals would be wealthier. Tax money that now goes to public schools and to clothing children could be converted to disposable income. Having plenty of time for exotic vacations and lots of money to pamper themselves, child-free couples would be more rested. If all went childless, North America would have an exceptionally productive, healthy, wealthy, and rested present—but no future.

Something very similar to this is happening in North America's churches: Foregoing parenting, our churches are exchanging the birthing of healthy new baby churches for their own prosperity at the present moment. My purpose in making this strong statement is not to condemn the efforts and priorities of our churches. Without question, our churches make a powerful and positive difference in individual lives and in communities. My hope, instead, is to start a conversation, a reevaluation of those priorities. I can hear the questions: How can our programs be productive if we send our most effective and compelling leaders away to pastor new churches? How can we breathe health and vitality into our ministries if we release perfectly good volunteers to serve baby congregations? Where do we find the wealth to finance our facilities if we give "the gift that keeps on giving," financial contributions of tithing congregants, to rent space for daughter churches? We are exhausted enough already just trying to minister to our own congregations; how can we minister effectively if we add the task of birthing new ones?

Questions like these demonstrate the enormity of the task at hand. Let us take a moment to address these questions by reflecting on some numbers that demonstrate where the North American church stands in the task of reaching our population with the gospel.

The Numbers

At a 2005 convention in Chicago two speakers were featured: Ted Haggard, the since-discredited then-president of the National Association of Evangelicals, and Ron Luce, the fiery director of Teen Mania, the organization that presents the popular "Acquire the Fire" stadium events. Haggard's message was affirming and comforting. Using George Barna's statistics to paint a picture of an expanding and successful evangelistic effort in the United States, his message could have been entitled, "Don't Worry; Be Happy." Luce's presentation, on the other hand, was intentionally disturbing. Fully intending to mobilize the two thousand or so pastors present in a strategic battle to win the hearts and minds of America's youth, Luce, quoting a since-challenged statistic,[6] declared that only 4 percent of the "rising generation"[7] are born-again Christians.

So who is right? Is Evangelical Christianity prospering, growing, and succeeding at making disciples of all nations, including this one? Or are we in a dire situation requiring urgent, focused action to keep the Christian faith from going the way of Zeus and Odin?

Answers to questions about the success or failure—growth or decline—of the Christian faith are exceptionally difficult to pin down conclusively: How is the genuineness of Christian faith

---

6 Laurie Goodstein, "Evangelicals Fear the Loss of Their Teenagers," *New York Times*, October 6, 2006. "Their alarm has been stoked by a *highly suspect* claim that if current trends continue, only 4 percent of teenagers will be 'Bible-believing Christians' as adults. That would be a sharp decline compared with 35 percent of the current generation of baby boomers, and before that, 65 percent of the World War II generation" italics mine.

7 Coral Ridge Presbyterian Church, "Children's Ministries," Coral Ridge Presbyterian Church, http://www.crpc.org/2000/Departments/Childrens%20Ministries/index.html (accessed December 8, 2006). Regarding the "rising generation," this very large church's Web site states, "These individuals (born between 1992 and 2005) number 72 million and are the second largest generation in the nation's history."

determined? Who makes the call? Should we count first-time faith confessions, born-again experiences, church membership roles, average weekly attendance figures, or attendance at peak times of the year? Should only Evangelical churches be counted, or should the mainline Protestant denominations be included? What about Catholics? Orthodox? Seventh Day Adventists? Mormons and Jehovah's Witnesses? Do we ask the churches or do we go directly to individuals and ask them?[8] Different studies use different criteria to answer these key questions.

The Ontario Consultants on Religious Tolerance contend that Christianity has fallen into decline in the United States:

> Large numbers of American adults are disaffiliating themselves from Christianity. ... *Identification with Christianity has suffered a loss of 9.7 percentage points in 11 years*—about 0.9 percentage points per year. This decline is identical to that observed in Canada between 1981 and 2001. If this trend continues, then by about the year 2042, non-Christians will outnumber the Christians in the U.S.[9]

---

8   Dale E. Jones et al., *Religious Congregations and Membership in the United States 2000* (Nashville, TN: Glenmary Research Center, 2002), xv–xvi. The problems noted in *Religious Congregations and Membership 2000* include: (1) "defining membership"—not all congregations acknowledge the idea of membership, and those that do use differing standards of membership; (2) "estimating total adherents"—some groups use this more broadly encompassing idea in place of membership; (3) "average attendance"—even weekly attendance-measuring methods differ significantly: for example, some groups count children while others do not; (4) "accuracy of reporting procedures"—this varies widely from group to group; and (5) "dual affiliation"—not only do some individuals belong to more than one congregation; but some congregations belong to more than one denomination!"
9   B. A. Robinson, "Religious Identification in the U.S.," Ontario Consultants on Religious Tolerance, http://www.religioustolerance.org/chr_prac2.htm (accessed April 25, 2006), italics mine.

The American Religious Identification Survey (ARIS) concludes that Americans are moving away from organized expressions of Christianity:[10]

> Often lost amidst the mesmerizing tapestry of faith groups ... is also a vast and growing population of *those without faith* ... The present survey has detected a wide and possibly growing swath of secularism among Americans.[11]

The Ontario Consultants and the authors of the ARIS report give credence to Luce's position. In contrast, George Barna's *The State of the Church: 2006*, concludes that the number of Christians in the United States is *not* in decline, but is at least stable and may be "hot."[12] Where the ARIS report uses self-identification to determine religious identification, this statistician of the born-again movement asks specific theological questions to determine if a person is truly an

---

10 Barry A. Kosmin, Egon Mayer, and Ariela Keysar, *American Religious Identification Survey 2001* (New York: City University of New York, Graduate Center, 2001), 7. One of the distinguishing features of this survey, like its 1990 predecessor, is that respondents were asked to describe themselves in terms of religion with an open-ended question. Interviewers did not prompt or offer a suggested list of potential answers. Moreover, the self-description of respondents was not based on whether established religious bodies, institutions, churches, mosques, or synagogues considered them to be members. Quite the contrary, the survey sought to determine whether the respondents themselves regarded themselves as adherents of a religious community. Subjective rather than objective standards of religious identification were tapped by the survey.
11 Ibid., 5–6, italics mine.
12 George Barna, *The State of the Church: 2006* (Ventura, CA: Barna Group, 2006), 50.

evangelical Christian.[13],[14] The percentage affirming "a personal commitment to Jesus Christ that is still important" and choosing the statement, "When you die you will go to heaven because you have confessed your sins and have accepted Jesus Christ as your savior," has increased steadily from 35 percent in 1991 to an amazing 45 percent in 2006.[15] Barna is clearly in Haggard's camp.

Their optimism, however, should be tempered by a key observation in a study by David Olson, a leading expert in church-multiplication associated with the Evangelical Covenant. Olson brings into consideration a phenomenon called the "halo effect" that occurs when people are asked to self-report on

13   Ibid., 29. The following questions are used to establish "born-again" status: Question 1: "Have you ever made a personal commitment to Jesus Christ that is still important in your life today?" Question 2: "I'm going to read some statements about what will happen to you after you die … Which one of those comes closest to what you believe? 1. When you die you will go to Heaven because you have tried to obey the Ten Commandments. 2. When you die you will go to Heaven because you are basically a good person. 3. When you die you will go to Heaven because you have confessed your sins and have accepted Jesus Christ as your savior. 4. When you die you will go to Heaven because God loves all people and will not let them perish. 5. When you die you will not go to Heaven. 6. You do not know what will happen after you die." If a person answers in the affirmative to question #1 and chooses option 3 for question #2, he or she is considered by the Barna team to be a born-again Christian.

14   Ibid., 14. The number of people affirming the theological statement "God is the all-powerful, all-knowing, perfect creator of the universe who rules the world today" over more generic ideas of the nature of God has remained stable within one percentage point since the Barna Group began asking the question in 1996. Barna's survey may be flawed in regard to this question because the response quoted above is worded in a much more compelling manner than any of the other options. It has the ring of a "right" answer when compared to the rest. For example, one of the other responses reads, "God refers to the total realization of personal, human potential."

15   Ibid., 29. "Numerically, this 45 percent is the equivalent of about 101 million born-again adults—the first time that the estimated number of born again adults has topped the 100 million mark."

personal issues like church attendance, voting, and smoking.[16] The number of people actually counted in churches on a given Sunday morning differs from the number of people who tell telephone survey workers that they attend church on Sunday mornings. According to Olson, "Numbers from actual counts of people in orthodox Christian churches show that 20.4 percent of the population attended church on any given weekend in 1990. That percentage dropped to 18.7 percent by 2000."[17] Olson's conclusions are based on the data of the Glenmary Study,[18] which evaluated reports from about 250,000 of the 350,000 churches in the United States, and must be considered much more conclusive than Barna's observations, which come from telephone interviews of only 1,002 adults.[19]

The number of church attendees has indeed risen from 50,848,000 to 52,500,000 between 1990 and 2000—an increase of just over 3 percent. In the same period, however, U.S. population has risen 13 percent.[20] Church attendance growth lags a full 10 percent behind! In fact, as a percentage of population growth, church attendance declined from 1990 to 2000 in every state of the union except Hawaii.

Remarkably, *all* numeric growth in U.S. church attendance is in the evangelical sector. Mainline Protestant and Roman Catholic church attendance figures are down significantly in

16   David T. Olson, *The State of the American Church* (The American Church, 2004), Slide 6. "People present themselves as having engaged in activities that make themselves look better to their peer group than they really are."
17   Ibid.
18   Jones et al, *Religious Congregations and Membership in the United States 2000*, xvi. These authors reported thirty-nine U.S. counties in which self-reported church membership *exceeded the total population of the county!* Of the three possible explanations the authors put forth, "church membership overcount" seems to be by far the most likely culprit. The other two explanations are "U.S Census undercount" and "county of residence differing from county of membership."
19   Barna, *The State of the Church: 2006*, 58.
20   Olson, *The State of the American Church*, Slide 10.

the United States. C. Kirk Hadaway reports, "Using adjusted membership figures, the Episcopal Church lost 829,000 active members between 1967 and 2002."[21] These losses seem moderate in comparison to those of other mainline churches. The Presbyterian Church (USA) lost an incredible 1.7 percent of its total membership in 2002 alone. The Church of Christ lost over 2 percent that same year![22]

Canadian losses exceed the losses in the United States, *Canadian Social Trends 2006* concludes, "The proportion of adult Canadians who either have no religious affiliation or do have a religion but don't attend religious services increased from 31 percent to 43 percent."[23]

These figures represent an annual disaffiliation rate with Christianity of over 0.5 percent per year, and they fail to take into account the difference between the religious practices of immigrants and Canadian-born citizens. Immigrants are much more likely to practice a religion other than Christianity. The index of religiosity among *immigrants* in Canada shows stable participation in spiritual disciplines and weekly attendance, which may indicate that non-Christian religions are holding

---

21   C. Kirk Hadaway, *Is the Episcopal Church Growing (or Declining)?* (New York: Episcopal Church Center, 2005), 6.

22   Ibid., 11.

23   Susan Crompton et al, *Canadian Social Trends 2006* (Ottawa, ON: Statistics Canada, 2006), 2. "Between 1985 and 2004, the share of Canadians aged 15 and older reporting no religious affiliation increased by seven percentage points from 12 percent to 19 percent. In addition, a growing share of Canadians had not attended any religious services in the previous year, even though they reported an affiliation (19 percent to 25 percent). *Canadian Social Trends 2006* explains their approach as follows: "An index of religiosity is developed based on the presence of religious affiliation, frequency of attendance at religious services, frequency of private religious practices and the importance of religion to the respondent." In this regard CST 2006 is quite helpful. Unfortunately, though, it does not explicitly differentiate between the religious practices of Christianity and those of other religions like Hinduism and Islam, which are increasingly prominent in Canada.

their own, but Christianity is in serious decline.[24] This outpacing of the growth of Christianity by other religions is not only a Canadian phenomenon; it is observed in study after study of church attendance in the United States.[25] Note the conclusion of researchers Carl Dudley and David Roozen: "The founding of congregations among Bahá'is, Muslims, and Mormons over the last twenty years ... is rapidly putting a new face on American religion."[26]

Based on the accumulated evidence cited, I am going to have to side with Luce. We are not in a "Don't Worry; Be Happy" moment in North American Christian history. Action is needed. But what kind of action? I propose the following: *North America's churches must ignite a parent-church movement.* Individual congregations in the United States must begin to see the birthing of new churches according to the parenting metaphor as a natural part of their church life cycle. Genuine parental nurture must be invested in every new church project, resulting in healthy, thriving congregations and leaders.

Why New Churches?

Why parent new churches rather than simply improving the health and strength of existing ones? Urban church-multiplication pioneer Tim Keller answers this question with a provocative claim:

---

24   Ibid., 4.
25   Kosmin, Mayer, and Keysar, *American Religious Identification Survey 2001*, 9–10. "Between 1990–2001 the proportion of the newly enlarged Asian American population who are Christian has fallen from 63% to 43%, while those professing Asian religions (Buddhism, Hinduism, Islam, etc.) has risen from 15% to 28%. Thus, for example, there are more than three times as many Hindus in the U.S. today as there were in 1990."
26   Carl S. Dudley and David A. Roozen, *Faith Communities Today: A Report on Religion in the United States Today* (Hartford, CT: Hartford Institute for Religion Research, 2001), 11.

The vigorous, continual planting of new congregations is the single most crucial strategy for (1) the numerical growth of the Body of Christ in any city, and (2) the continual corporate renewal and revival of the existing churches in a city. Nothing else ... will have the consistent impact of dynamic, extensive church planting ... *The only way to truly be sure you are creating permanent new Christians is to plant churches.*[27]

Olson reinforces this conclusion: "Church planting is *the most powerful* growth mechanism for the American church."[28] This can be seen by comparing the contribution of new church development on total attendance to that of the growth of established churches.[29] In *only one* denomination does the growth of established churches exceed that of new churches. In all others—and as a whole—growth from new churches dwarfs that from established churches. In four out of nine denominations, *the only growth present at all is from new churches!*[30] Listen to Olson's complacency-shattering conclusion: "In this last decade, new churches were *23 times* more productive in producing attendance growth than established churches (of the 3 million more people in worship in 2000 than 1990, *96 percent of these came from new churches*)."[31]

---

27 Timothy J. Keller and J. Allen Thompson, *Church Planter Manual* (New York: Redeemer Church Planting Center, 2002), 29 italics mine. © Used by permission.

28 Olson, Slide 87, italics mine. "This presentation is based on a nationwide study of American Christian church attendance, as reported by churches and denominations. The database currently has average worship attendances for each of the last 10 years for over 170,000 individual churches throughout the country."

29 Stuart Murray, *Church Planting: Laying Foundations*, North American ed. (Scottdale, PA: Herald Press, 2001), 31.

30 Olson, *The State of the American Church*, Slide 111.

31 Ibid., Slide 122, italics mine.

The Metaphor: Parenting or Planting?

As we start new churches, are we planting plants or are we having babies? Since the 1990 publication of Wagner's *Church Planting for a Greater Harvest*, and even before, efforts in church-multiplication typically have been conducted under the metaphor of *planting*. Other metaphors can be detected in trace amounts—the construction metaphor in denominations that speak of "new church development"[32] or the cell mitosis metaphor in groups that speak of "church-multiplication"[33]— but none of these is nearly as widespread as planting. In the way Wagner intended it, as an *agricultural* metaphor, planting is not an inherently flawed way of looking at the establishment of new churches.[34] It could be that, in rural communities, planting is even the *best* metaphor. The challenge comes when this metaphor is transplanted into a suburban or urban context. What was meant as an agricultural metaphor quickly becomes a *residential landscaping* metaphor. Perhaps, at first hearing, this seems an insignificant difference, but the implications for establishing new congregations are genuine and profound. Since the vast majority of new church starts take place in non-

---

32 Presbyterian Church (USA), "New Church Development: Building the Church One Congregation at a Time," Presbyterian Church (USA), http://www.pcusa.org/newchurch/ (accessed November 29, 2006).
33 Church-multiplication Associates, "Welcome to Church-multiplication Associates," Church-multiplication Associates, http://www.cmaresources.org (accessed November 29, 2006). Even though CMA uses church-multiplication language, the planting metaphor permeates the language and graphics of their site.
34 It is important to acknowledge the gigantic debt the church-multiplication movement owes to C. Peter Wagner and his work. Tens of thousands of new churches have been started and hundreds of thousands of people have come to faith as a direct or indirect result of Wagner's influence. This work is presented in the hope that it will be received as a celebration of Wagner's leadership in the discipline of new church development—and as a continuation, extension, and refinement of the conversation that he began seventeen years ago.

agricultural communities, these implications appear in very real ways in real-life church starts.

Tom Nebel, who directs the church-multiplication efforts for the Baptist General Conference, in his very practical book *Big Dreams in Small Places*, observes, "The authors of church planting and church growth resources were suggesting that the best places, if not the only places, where God could start and grow churches were in growing urban and suburban environments."[35] The well-articulated premise of Nebel's work is that, when contrasted to small-town rural situations, it is much more difficult to establish new churches in suburban and, especially, urban contexts. This is certainly so. Nonetheless, a report by the Southern Baptist Convention's North American Mission Board (NAMB) shows that the cities and their metropolitan areas are, nonetheless, the most *fruitful* areas for new church starts.[36] So, for good or ill, we find ourselves speaking to urban and suburban church leaders with a rural metaphor that is too often misunderstood or misapplied.

Especially in suburban neighborhoods, we see *planting* as the process of going to the nursery, picking out a healthy young plant, digging a hole, improving the soil a little, adding fertilizer, putting the plant in the hole, adding some water, and walking away. It is the work of two or three hours on a Saturday afternoon. The plant may never need care or maintenance again. If it does, the care may be limited to a little pruning every couple of years, maybe some watering in the dry season, perhaps a little fertilizer. By framing the establishment of new congregations under the rubric of residential landscaping, the

---

35   Thomas P. Nebel, *Big Dreams in Small Places* (St. Charles, IL: ChurchSmart, 2002), 18.

36   Edward J. Stetzer, *An Analysis of the Church Planting Process and Other Selected Factors on the Attendance of SBC Church Plants* (Alpharetta, GA: Southern Baptist Convention, 2003), 6. Stetzer includes a bar chart showing that the four most effective settings for new church starts are in suburban or urban contexts ("Large City Suburb," "Regional City/Downtown," "Mega City/Downtown," and "Mega City Suburb").

planting metaphor unintentionally creates the expectation in founding congregations that starting a new church requires little cost and effort, and that the new entity will become self-sustaining quickly. Planting as a metaphor for the starting of new churches suggests that what little investment is required will happen up front and will be over quickly.

Contrast this with a parenting metaphor. In parenting, the up-front investment at the conception stage is insignificant when compared to the effort expended later. The birthing stage is both painful and life consuming. All other activities stop for the coming of a baby. But that pain and the event of birth is not the end. It is only the beginning. The parents will soon learn that all aspects of their lives will be altered by the coming of that child—and, to a gradually decreasing degree, for the rest of their lives. They dedicate themselves to learning all they can about child rearing; all their evenings are busy; they do not have time for their old friends; any extra money goes into savings for college; all spare time is spent taking the kids to dance lessons, music classes, and team sports. In the end, though, despite the immeasurable investment, the very fact of the child's existence gives meaning to the parents' life.

Planting begins at noon and ends at 3:00 pm. Parenting begins at conception and, though it may decrease significantly in intensity about nineteen or twenty years later, it never really ends. If children were treated like landscape plants, they would die quickly of exposure and starvation. Why do we expect a different result for baby churches? Just as human parenting is simultaneously the most costly and the most rewarding endeavor a couple will ever undertake, *parenting* new congregations should be similarly the most costly and the most rewarding investment a church will ever make.

A Parent-Church Culture

It is a common staple in books on church-multiplication to propose and contrast varieties of models—a practice characterized by remarkable breadth and variety. British author Stuart Murray discusses colonization, planting teams, planting via social action, satellite planting, and planting by adoption.[37] Among Southern Baptist leader Ed Stetzer's models are the apostolic harvest church, the founding pastor model, and the team planting model.[38] Tim Keller presents three practical models: urban regional crossroads, targeted toward urban professionals; parish-based, addressing the poor; and multicultural, appealing to immigrants and the ethnic grassroots.[39]

Wagner differentiates between "modality" models, conceived and carried out by a local church, and "sodality" models, devised and executed by a denominational agency or para-church organization.[40] The variety of models is limited only by the creativity and imagination of church leaders. While some models are more conducive to involvement from a mother church than others (obviously, Wagner's sodality models exclude such involvement by definition), my purpose is not to emphasize one model over others, but to advocate for a culture—a *mode*, or *mind-set*—in church-multiplication that includes a high level of involvement by the pastor(s), staff, lay leadership, and congregation of the mother church. This might be expressed in Wagner's hiving-off model, in Keller's urban regional crossroads model, or in Murray's colonization or satellite models. The parent/child relationship need not be model specific. What is of utmost importance is that the involvement and investment of the parenting church be more than "in name only."[41] The parenting church should carry out its role in the life

37   Murray, *Church Planting*, 235–250.
38   Stetzer, *Planting New Churches*, 49–69.
39   Keller and Thompson, *Church Planter Manual*, 53–56.
40   Wagner, *Church Planting for a Greater Harvest*, 59–60.
41   Stetzer, *Analysis of the Process*, 20.

of the new church the way wise, loving human parents invest in the life of *their* child—church *reproduction* with a parenting mind-set ... or, perhaps even better, a parenting *heart*-set.

As the culture and practices inherent in the metaphor of church parenting increase, there will be at least two powerful benefits to the church-multiplication movement in North America: First, local churches will begin to see themselves as the primary engines of church-multiplication, thereby increasing the quantity of new church starts. Second, as newly birthed churches have the advantage of deeper and more meaningful nurturance by parent congregations operating under the parent-church mind-set, their vitality, longevity, and impact will rise, thereby improving the success rate of church-multiplication attempts.

Increase the Quantity

As congregations take primary ownership of the mission away from denominational agencies, our churches will no longer think of the establishment of new congregations as somebody else's problem. One hundred forty-nine denominations encompass almost three-quarters of the congregations in North America,[42] and only a fraction of these have the combination of a motivating vision and an effective strategy for church-multiplication. There are, by contrast, over 300,000 *congregations.*[43] By transferring the responsibility for starting new churches from denominations to congregations, as the parenting metaphor naturally and logically does, we multiply the number of potential parents by almost 2,000! If we aspire, as Olson suggests, to increase our

---

42   B. A. Robinson, "Christian Meta-Groups, Wings, Families, Denominations, Faith Groups, & Belief Systems," Ontario Consultants on Religious Tolerance, http://www.religioustolerance.org/christ7.htm (accessed December 20, 2006). There are approximately twelve hundred total denominations in North America.

43   Olson, *The State of the American Church*, Slide 6.

church birth rate from 3,800 to 6,900 per year, we need more parents!

Of course, a denomination holds the potential to be a much more prolific parent than does an individual congregation. It is also true that denominations have several ongoing roles in church-multiplication: setting policy; establishing guidelines; and providing assessment, training, auxiliary funding, pre-birth "boot camps," and coaching services. In order to meet Olson's challenging annual goal, between 10 and 15 percent of existing congregations would have to commit to birthing *one new congregation every five years.*[44] The need for existing churches to serve as the engines of church-multiplication has long been recognized. In 1980, Donald McGavran wrote, "Part of your congregation's mission lies in the sponsorship of still more congregations."[45]

Improve the Vitality

Aside from vastly improving the numeric base of potential parents, the parenting metaphor offers another significant intrinsic benefit: if sponsoring congregations hold in their collective minds and hearts the picture of nurturance by loving parents—and commit themselves to fulfilling the basic commitments of weekly supervision and coaching, core group members, and appropriate financing—the success rate of new churches will rise dramatically. Infant mortality will fall as neo-natal care improves. The metaphor of parenting, followed to its logical conclusions, will result in a dramatic improvement in the health of our church-multiplication efforts and their leaders, and will motivate more local congregations to engage in the missional practice of establishing new congregations.

---

44   See Appendix A: "Project One-Five."
45   Donald A. McGavran and George G Hunter III, *Church Growth Strategies That Work*, Creative Leadership Series, ed. Lyle E. Schaller (Nashville, TN: Abingdon, 1980), 99.

Hazards Inherent in Planting

Murray warns against the shortsighted establishment of new churches that often results from the mind-set subconsciously communicated by the planting metaphor:

> Attempting to plant churches quickly to achieve ... short-term goals may result in the planting of weak churches, with inadequately trained leaders, the shortcomings of which may discourage further church planting ... Such church planting ... may have the potential actually to set back the fulfillment of the Great Commission by increasing the alienation of certain sectors of society.[46]

Stetzer demonstrates that inattention or insufficient attention by the sponsoring church is a problem in church starts from "the words of church planters themselves":

> Church planters feel that they are "dropped in the middle of nowhere with no further contact."
>
> Mother churches need to be better trained and motivated in order to be more involved in the daughter church.
>
> Financial challenges were frequently overwhelming. Very few churches became self-supporting before ... funding ended.[47]

Asked, "What were the three most important things you wish you knew before you planted?" two of the most frequent responses of pioneer pastors were: "That *commitment from the mother church would be in name only*;" and "That *contact with* [supporting

---

46   Murray, *Church Planting*, 101.
47   Stetzer, *Analysis of the Process*, 20.

organizations]*would practically cease to exist* once [the pastor] arrived on the field."[48]

Stetzer concludes, "Church planter support systems are lacking and need to be readdressed."[49] Murray adds credence to Stetzer's contention that our present planting-based policies are putting too much stress on pioneer pastors:

> I regularly receive telephone calls from people I have never met, desperate for help in situations where church planting seems to have turned sour ... most have encountered difficulties related to unclear vision, insecure foundations, unrealistic expectations, inadequate leadership, limited training, and lack of ongoing supervision.[50]

The mixed success of efforts to establish new churches under the planting metaphor has dampened the spirits of some potential mother church pastors, bringing about a de-motivating level of skepticism among many. Why? They have experienced the disappointment and disillusionment of pioneer pastors who have tried and failed to establish new works—not to mention members of their congregation who often end up burned out, used up, and cynical of new efforts.[51] They have seen the negative effect that a failed work can have on the fertility of a particular field as multiple church planting attempts come through, each one over promising and under delivering.[52] They

---

48   Ibid., italics mine.
49   Ibid., 21.
50   Murray, *Church Planting*, 17–18.
51   Ibid. "I am troubled by the many conversations I have had with men and women involved in church plants that are struggling, failing to thrive, or on the point of closing. I regularly receive telephone calls from people I have never met, desperate for help in situations where church planting seems to have turned sour."
52   Ibid., 101–102. "Such church planting ... may have the potential actually to set back the fulfillment of the Great Commission by increasing

have seen church plants with very limited success that create only struggling, under-funded congregations with little real vision and even less ability to accomplish what vision they do have.[53] The kinds of problems I have just referenced are inherent in the landscaping metaphor of church *planting*.

Conclusion

The high incidence of pioneer-pastor burnout and new-church failure is due, at least in significant measure, to broad reliance on the faulty and insufficient metaphor of church *planting*. We need to shed this metaphor and adopt a better one, lest Murray's ominous warning prove true in North America as he contends it has in the United Kingdom, "The planting of yet more churches which damage their most committed members, and further alienate those beyond the reach of existing churches, will hinder rather than advance God's mission."[54]

Let us listen again to the questions I asked at the beginning of this chapter: How can our programs be productive if we send our most effective and compelling leaders away to pastor new churches? How can we breathe health and vitality into our ministries if we release perfectly good volunteers to serve baby congregations? Where do we find the wealth to finance our facilities if we give "the gift that keeps on giving"—financial contributions of tithing congregants—to rent space for daughter churches? We are exhausted enough already just trying to minister to our own people, how can we minister effectively if we add the task of birthing new congregations? Perhaps the best

---

the alienation of certain sectors of society from a church that appears to be even more firmly wedded to sectors to which they find it hard to identify."

53 Ibid., 27. "There are situations where a relatively strong and healthy church has planted a new congregation that has failed to thrive and where, two or three years later, there are fewer people in the two congregations than there were in the original congregation."

54 Ibid., 159.

way to answer these questions is to hear the story of a pastor who chose to make these exact sacrifices for the sake of the Great Commission and the Kingdom of Heaven.

Mother Church Story—Visionary Leadership

Background

A pioneer in the late-twentieth-century church-multiplication movement, the recently retired Dr. Jan Hettinga, served as senior pastor of Northshore Baptist Church, a highly respected anchor church in the Seattle region with average Sunday attendance of about twenty-five hundred. Located in Bothell, Washington, a suburb northeast of Seattle, Northshore Baptist has parented five congregations, resulting in a vibrant and effective network of churches birthing churches. Northshore is now a great-grandparent over a family of churches ministering to nearly five thousand people each Sunday. I interviewed Dr. Hettinga in his office at Northshore Baptist in January of 2007. Here are his words:

Interview Excerpts: Dr. Jan Hettinga

Church planting lore was just taking off in the early nineties. Our denomination promoted church planting, but they had stopped putting dollars toward it and really it wasn't anybody's responsibility. We realized that, if we were going to see new churches started, we were going to have to do it ourselves. We began preparing for that: I started preaching about church-multiplication. The buzz in the staff was, "Hey, we're going to plant a church."

I had a young guy on staff who had lots of promise: entrepreneurial to the core, one of the best communicators I had ever heard. By 1992, this young pastor was ready—more than ready, he was eager. We sent him and his wife to one of the first church planters' assessment centers. They came back with huge kudos. What happened was, this young guy was such a marketing guru, he wanted to do something quite different. He had a vision for the "weekenders." The statistics told us that one third of the people of the Seattle region were out of town on any given weekend. They're at their cabins. They're skiing. His big idea was to have a service that caught these folks before they left town: a Thursday night service. About fifty people formed a core group from Northshore. A number of them were really good leaders: small group leaders, worship people, teachers.

They first met in a daycare center and got off to a bang. They had one hundred fifty people their first few weeks. It became apparent that they were catching the twentysomethings—primarily because the worship was pretty edgy and the pastor was an innovative communicator. When the funding ran out, though, they no longer had enough to rent the daycare center. So we invited them back here, thinking that would give them a run at becoming self-sufficient. His one hundred fifty dwindled to one hundred, and then to seventy. When he hit fifty-five adults—without talking to me—he pulled the plug. It was pretty discouraging for the whole church to have a two-and-a-half-year-old die. Yet, out of it, God rebuilt the vision.

Next time we planted two churches at the same time. New Song, a plant in Bellevue-Redmond, had a ten-year run—a solid church for probably eight or nine years. The other twin that went out along with New Song was Cascade Community Church in Monroe, which has boomed. It became very effective in the harvest—hundreds and hundreds of people have come to Christ there—and it is now a mother church in its own right, working on its fifth daughter church. They are going to be a grandparent—and we're going to be a great-grandparent.

The most critical thing that I have learned is how important the right leader is. A lot of people feel that they could plant a church, but it's actually a pretty rare bird that does it well. As we've gone on, we've become more careful about who we put weight down on. The other thing is the coaching. The one thing that Nate got—my son, who is the pastor at Cascade in Monroe—was a lot of my time and attention. He was not averse to coming to me for advice, whereas some of the other guys just felt as if I might not have time for them.

When it comes right down to paying the cost of planting a daughter church, it can seem like a distraction, competitive with other priorities. From a human perspective, it does look like an impractical idea. In the end, when you step out in faith, God rewards your generosity. You're opening your hand and letting God take good people—good leaders—but that new congregation is more productive at reaching lost people than the older congregation. Every time Northshore has planted, we have been in a building project. The money came in, the project was completed, and, at the same time, another church was started. The same is true with leaders. In a large church like this, there is a glass ceiling. Really good leaders show up, but there is no place for them to serve. So, when you can open your hand and release those new leaders to new churches, it's a win-win for the Kingdom. Plus, if some of your leaders go—every time we've planted a church we've lost staff members and elders—then there are new places to fill here, and new blood and new ideas and new energy roll in.

Within the last ten years, Northshore could have moved out a ways further, bought some acreage, and rebuilt the campus that we're now on. Instead, we decided to stay in this neighborhood and grow by multiplying churches. We have about twenty-five hundred for our weekend services. We are now the minority. There are more people meeting outside in the daughter, granddaughter, and great-granddaughter churches than are meeting here—about fifty-five hundred plus! We have a potluck dinner in the fall called "Homecoming." All of the pastors, elders, board members, and their wives come together for an exchange of stories. It was magnificent this year! We had more stories of people coming to Christ! Our congregation really sees church-multiplication as part of our self-image—our

DNA. All the leaders own it; the staff members own it. We look at it as having started something that now is released to the Spirit—and God has got something rolling—that snowball rolling downhill that keeps growing as it rolls.

CHAPTER 2
TAKING STOCK: A LOOK BACK

*Fresh ventures to evangelize ... will require the replacement
of these [previously failed] churches with new ones, but this
is likely to succeed only if the reasons for past failures are
understood and addressed.*[55]

—*Stuart Murray*

Mike and Donna set out to start a new church. They had funding
from the denomination. They had training. They had potential.
They even had a few people and some equipment. But twelve
months and two locations later, they left the work and closed
the church, disillusioned and a little bitter. Their core had not
grown as they had hoped, they had failed to see the evangelistic
numbers they imagined, and the new church had never become
financially viable. Eventually, most of their congregation had
drifted back to the mother church, or maybe they were not in
church at all anymore. If you have been in ministry leadership
for long, you likely know people like Mike and Donna. Perhaps
they are part of your congregation even now.

Stories of results like these may be the reason you have
never taken seriously enough your denomination's church-

---

55   Murray, *Church Planting*, 91. © Used by permission.

multiplication efforts and sent people out to start a church. Though you may not be sufficiently cynical to speak the words out loud, inwardly you ask, *Who decided that the world needs another tiny, struggling, under- funded, ineffective church anyway?* In conversation after conversation with potential mother church pastors, I have come to believe that this unspoken question is lying just below the surface, and not without reason! Starting new churches is exceptionally challenging work and it takes a toll on people—even in successful works.

Perils and Misconceptions

Author Stuart Murray demonstrates remarkable insight and candor in addressing some common church-multiplication perils and misconceptions:

> The establishing of a new congregation is a penultimate rather than ultimate goal.[56]

> Church planting is not an end in itself, because the church is an agent of God's mission.[57]

> Church planting does not ensure that the churches planted will be any more successful in avoiding self-absorption and a maintenance mentality than other churches.[58]

> Indeed, there are situations where a new church has quickly become more introverted and less potent evangelistically than the church from which it was planted.[59]

---

56 Ibid., 31.
57 Ibid., 40.
58 Ibid., 31.
59 Ibid., 127.

Church planting that fails to engage with the mission agenda of Jesus can easily become church centered rather than Kingdomoriented.[60]

The multiplication of churches characterized by racism or sexism may contribute to church growth but also represent a strengthening of forces opposed to God's rule of justice and peace.[61]

Sectarian planting ... merely rearranges the Christian community, rather than making further disciples, and ... may actually diminish the church's impact and witness.[62]

Attempting to plant churches quickly ... may result in the planting of weak churches, with inadequately trained leaders, the shortcomings of which may discourage further church planting.[63]

Murray's concerns fall into three categories: church-multiplication as a theologically secondary issue; the difficulty of ensuring an outwardly focused, missional character in new congregations; and the possibility that new works will fail to thrive. Since the third consideration is the subject of the next chapter, let us explore Murray's first two concerns here.

Theology

Theologically, the propagation of new churches is not a secondary issue, as Murray asserts; it is a *tertiary* activity. First is the Kingdom of Heaven, second is evangelism, and third is the establishment of churches. The Kingdom of Heaven is the message, the ultimate reality into which God

---

60 Ibid., 43.
61 Ibid., 49–50.
62 Ibid., 96.
63 Ibid., 101.

beckons. Evangelism is the proclamation of that message and reality. The church is the transformative context and divinely ordained community in which the encounter with the Kingdom of Heaven is embodied and lived out. In the New Testament, the establishment of new churches was a response to God's activity in and through the evangelists rather than an initiative in its own right. When Peter stood up to preach at nine o'clock that morning in Jerusalem, he did not turn to the men and women with whom he had been praying in the upper room and say, "Watch this. I'm going to start a church." There was no church-multiplication strategy. There was no proposal or assessment. In an act of Spirit-inspired evangelism, he simply preached the Kingdom of Heaven in a way that was significant and appropriate to that place and that moment in history. The formation of Jerusalem's first mega-church was simply the gathering of those who responded to evangelistic proclamation into a Christ-centered, communal embodiment of the gospel message. This *proclaim-and-gather* model seems to be the most prominent New Testament paradigm: Initiated by God and inspired by the message, "Repent, for the Kingdom of Heaven is at hand," someone preaches the gospel. Those who respond are then gathered into transformative Christian community. *Evangel, kerygma, ekklessia*: Gospel, proclamation, church. This was the model in Jerusalem (Acts 2). This was the model in Philippi (Acts 16:13–15), in Thessalonica (Acts 17:1–15), and probably also in Corinth (Acts 18:1–11).

The other prominent New Testament church-multiplication model differs slightly from the proclaim-and-gather model. It might be called the *involuntary relocation* model, where persecution forced the church to scatter, and, like dandelion seeds blown by the wind, communities of Christians landed in previously un-evangelized communities. This is evidenced in Phillip's involuntary relocation to Samaria (Acts 8:4–8), is certainly the origin of the church in Antioch (Acts 11:19–21), seems to be the pattern in Ephesus (Acts 19:1, "There he found some disciples"), and is most likely how the church in Rome came to be.

These two models have at least two important features in common: (1) the initiative was God's and, (2) the establishment of churches was in response to effective evangelism. This pattern can be seen in Paul's instructions to Titus: "I left you in Crete ... that you might put in order what was left unfinished and appoint elders in every town." Titus' role brought structure and leadership to the community in Crete that came into being as an ingathering of those who responded to the evangelistic proclamation of the gospel: *Evangel, kerygma, ekklessia*: Gospel, proclamation, church.

What do we do with all this? One key application is this: Send pastors out to start new churches only if they are verifiably effective, proven evangelists. There is a myth in church planting lore: "If the pastor is not an evangelist, just make sure that someone on his team is." Do not believe it. If a new church is to thrive, whoever is preaching must be able to evangelize with consistent effectiveness. Having a non-senior-pastor evangelist taking care of babies in the nursery, teaching Sunday school class, running sound, or sitting in the congregation listening to Greek-heavy, academic sermons simply will not do. The evangelist must evangelize. Without evangelists *at the helm*, new church efforts will fail to thrive.

Of course, a non-evangelistically gifted pastor can be effective in many roles. An established church may benefit to a greater degree from leadership by a pastor with strong counseling, teaching, or administrative gifts than they would from an evangelist. An evangelist may be seen as a troublemaker in these contexts, moving forward with radical ideas before winning the trust of key lay leaders. Growth in congregational size, however, is not essential to pastoral success in an established church as it is in a pioneer work. If a flourishing church with weekly attendance of 350 experiences no numerical growth, it remains a church of 350. But, if a core group starts out with ten members, hoping to become a flourishing congregation of 350, and experiences no numerical growth, they will become a disillusioned bunch of people wondering why God failed to come through for them.

In church-planter assessment interviews, it is common to ask: "What redemptive relationships do you have with unchurched people?" A good question, but not good enough. The question needs to be: "Who have you led to a saving knowledge of Jesus Christ and how did it happen?" If the candidate cannot name names, tell stories, and give timelines, redirect him or her to other kinds of ministry.

This brings us back to Mike and Donna's story. One key reason that some new church efforts falter is that they attempt to multiply churches without the essential aspect of evangelistic gospel proclamation. They send out leaders whose primary gifts are teaching and pastoral care to do an evangelistic task. What do they get? Small, stagnant groups of well-educated, thoroughly counseled, but very frustrated Christians. They thought they were launching a church; they were actually supplying an unemployed pastor with a pulpit.

When Peter preached on Pentecost morning, perhaps his mind went back to his encounter with Jesus recorded in Matthew 16. A tiny fragment of this conversation is commonly cited in church planting boot camps and intensives to motivate new church-multiplication efforts. We show the "If you build it, they will come" clip from *Field of Dreams*,[64] then excerpt "I will build my church" out of the middle of Matthew 16:18—a motivating combination, but one with unfortunate consequences. Some conclude from this passage that, if they establish new churches, people will automatically flock to them and fill them up. For the sake of clarity and theological precision, let us take a closer look at this most controversial of biblical passages:

---

64 *Field of Dreams*, directed by Phil Alden Robinson, Universal Pictures, 1989.

Jesus ... asked his disciples, "Who do you say I am?" Simon Peter answered, "You are the Messiah, the Son of the living God." Jesus replied, "Blessed are you, Simon son of Jonah, for this was not revealed to you by flesh and blood, but by my Father in heaven. And I tell you that you are Peter, and on this rock I will build my church, and the gates of death will not overcome it." (Matthew 16:13–18)

Immediately, we can assert two propositions confidently: First, God's church is built by Jesus as the prime actor: "*I* will build my church." Second, the church ultimately belongs to Jesus: "I will build *my* church."

A third important conclusion is that God, in Jesus Christ, uses human agency to build his church. Simon Peter is one example, the first among many in whom this agency could and would reside. The prime qualification for God's selection of those he invites into this role is the possession of a clear and profound understanding of the person of Jesus as the Messiah and Son of God. This interpretation is *not* contingent upon the conviction that the antecedent of *petra* ("rock" in verse 18) is Peter's confession, "You are the Messiah, the Son of the living God" (verse 16), rather than Peter's name *petros* (which is the most intuitive and grammatically satisfying choice). Even if it is assumed that the antecedent of *petra* is *petros*, Peter can still be seen as a figure representing many who will make a similar confession. The confession, therefore, remains determinative in God's choice of church-building agents.

All who make the Christian confession, "You are the Messiah, the Son of the living God" (and does this not include all who may rightly be called Christians?) are invited by God to join Jesus in building the Christian church.

So far, then, we have four conclusions:

1. Jesus is the initiator and prime actor in the project of building the church.

2. The church being built belongs to Jesus.
3. Jesus employs human agency in the process of building his church.
4. The criterion for invitation into this agency role is the Christian confession, "You are the Messiah, the Son of the living God."

Before it is appropriate to conclude that this passage is rightly used to assure success in the propagation of new churches, let us pay attention to one additional aspect of verse 18: What does it mean to *build*? The Greek term translated as build is *oikodomeo*, to construct, to build up or to reinforce. Notice that there are at least two primary concepts: initial construction and continued strengthening. Since no church existed at the time that these words recorded in Matthew were spoken, Jesus' use clearly includes the initial act of bringing the church into existence, but it seems unlikely that his intent was limited to the groundbreaking stage. Matthew chose to include this *pericope* to encourage, or build up, the church of his own day, thirty or forty years after the events recorded and after the founding of the Jerusalem church at Pentecost.

Given this semantic range, the best understanding of this conversation between Simon Peter and Jesus is as follows: Every Christian ought to participate in Jesus' purpose to increase the Christian church's size, range, scope, health, and strength. This should occur in a manner consistent with each individual's spiritual giftedness, according to means directed by the Holy Spirit, and informed by experience, experimentation, and study by those who have gone before.

Jesus' words to Peter in verse 18 should not be understood as a mandate compelling Peter toward some course of action. They are, instead, an expression of Jesus' intent to himself act in a way that will result in his church being built. Peter, and those who share his confession regarding the Messianic role and divine origin of Jesus, will somehow be involved, but in a non-initiatory role—Jesus is the primary and ultimate initiator. This passage is not a mandate to start new churches; less still is it a promise that those planted will magically fill with people. It is simply an invitation to those who confess Christ to participate with Jesus in his global and universal project of constructing, building up, remodeling, and reinforcing his church until the culmination of the "church age." Starting new churches is part of this project and must be done. It should, however, be done with great care, planning, and nurturance.

Outward Focus

Another of the real-life concerns expressed by Murray is that new churches may turn out to be no more missional or outwardly focused than their mother churches. This can be addressed fairly succinctly with two observations: First, the fact that the mother church decided to take the costly step of parenting a new church is a clear real-world demonstration of a missional, outwardly focused heart. Mother churches are, by definition, missional. Otherwise, they would have simply continued to invest in their own programs. The intent of Murray's statement must be to suggest that congregations often lose missional focus before they reach the later stages of the ministry life cycle. This is true to some degree, but it must be conceded that churches that actively choose to parent new churches thereby manifest a missional focus. This means that a missional focus is passed on in the DNA of the baby church.

Second, it does not follow that the baby church will immediately begin to manifest this missional focus. How many unselfish, giving, outwardly focused babies do you know? A human infant requires an external source of care and nurturance. If this care and nurturance are given, along with godly teaching and parental coaching, the child will eventually grow to be a giving, considerate, mature contributor. My wife and I have four primary goals for our children: that they will love and serve God, that they will know they are loved, that they will love and respect us as parents, and that they will contribute something positive to the world. We were not, however, idealistic enough to expect that all these things would be true of them when they were still infants in diapers! Why would anybody expect this of baby churches? Of course the goal is to establish missional churches that love God, are confident in God's love, receive nurture from their parent churches, and contribute something positive to the world.

Floyd Tidsworth, an expert on congregational life cycle, identifies six stages through which a young, healthy church typically progresses: "discovery, preparation, cultivation, fellowship, mission, and church."[65] Notice that mission, the first stage involving outward focus, does not occur until the *fifth* out of six phases. The familiar stages in classic team development theory, originally proposed in 1965 by Bruce Tuckman, are: forming, storming, norming, performing, and adjourning and transforming.[66] Notice that the productive stage, *performing*, is preceded by three other stages. I wonder why we expect new churches to reach full productivity immediately. We do not expect it of children. We do not expect it of corporations. Instead, we can create strategies for birthing new churches that allow them to be nursed and diapered in their early days, so that they can safely and naturally mature, eventually reaching fully missional, outwardly focused ministry productivity.

I do not want to leave you with the impression that Stuart Murray stands as a critic of the church-multiplication movement. He is a practitioner and a long-time leader who wishes to improve future efforts by taking a realistic look at the past:

---

65   Floyd Tidsworth, *Life Cycle of a New Congregation* (Nashville, TN: Broadman Press, 1992), xii.
66   Bruce Tuckman, "Developmental Sequence in Small Groups," *Psychological Bulletin* 63 (1965).

Self-propagation, or reproduction, is not just an admirable quality of some churches, but integral to the definition of the church.[67]

Reproductive churches can impart much to the churches they bring to birth, but church planting is also an opportunity for their own renewal.[68]

Church planting may be peripheral theologically by comparison with a theme like the Kingdom of God, but it is the primary context within which the New Testament was written, and by reference to which it should be understood.[69]

The planting of new churches has the potential to recall local churches to their essential task of mission.[70]

Hurdles

Before moving on, it is important to discuss two of the major hurdles that must be cleared if efforts to expand the Kingdom through the parenting of new churches are to succeed: the closure of existing churches and survival rates of new church starts.

Closure of Existing Churches

The very first hurdle in the multiplication race is the need to compensate for church closures. Simply to maintain a stable number of worshiping communities, we must launch a sufficient number of new congregations to replace those that

---

67   Murray, *Church Planting*, 64. © Used by permission.
68   Ibid., 61.
69   Ibid., 80.
70   Ibid., 109.

close. One example that illustrates this point comes from the International Church of the Foursquare Gospel, a denomination with a reputation for aggressive church planting. Between 2001 and 2005, Foursquare established 648 new churches in the United States, thereby increasing their total U.S. church count by seventy-four! What happened to the other 574? They were offset by church closures. For the past five years, Foursquare has closed over 6 percent of existing churches each year.[71] Assuming this trend continues, Foursquare must establish 115 new congregations each year in the United States to compensate for closures.

Foursquare is not alone. Olson observed in 2004, "In this decade, approximately 3,000 churches closed every year." This means that three thousand new congregations must be started every year—just to keep up! "While more churches were started, only 3,800 survived." The net gain, so far in the twenty-first century, has been only 800 churches per year. Perhaps this number sounds acceptable at first. An *Outreach Magazine* special report, however, makes the following salient observation: "From 2000 to 2004, a net gain of 13,024 churches was necessary to keep up with the U.S. population growth. In reality, that means rather than growing with the population, the Church *incurred a deficit of almost 10,000 churches.*"[72] Olson believes that, in order to reverse the present trend, congregations and denominations must set an annual pace of

---

71   Olson, *The State of the American Church*, Slides 79–81. Olson cites an annual closure figure of 6.8 percent for Foursquare, which at first looks quite discouraging. He goes on to say, "There is a 'counter-intuitive' observation ... The higher the closure rate, the faster the growth of the denomination; the lower the closure rate, the more likely it is to be declining. This happens because groups that are more aggressive in church planting are willing to take more risk and have many more young churches that might close."

72   Rebecca Barnes and Lindy Lowry, "Special Report: The American Church in Crisis," *Outreach Magazine* (May/June 2006), 103, italics mine.

6,900 new churches in the United States each year, a scenario he considers unlikely.[73]

Survival Rates

The second hurdle is the survival rates of the new churches. If the majority of closing churches were fifty-year-old congregations that had healthy life cycles of fruitfully transforming and enriching the people and communities they served, then declined as their membership aged and died off, that might be an acceptable situation. If they, on the other hand, represent attempted new church starts that struggled along for one, three, five, or ten years, never reaching real ministry fruitfulness, then closed because the congregation's tenacity was finally strained beyond the breaking point, that would be much more serious. Acknowledging that "new church closure figures can be slippery,"[74] Olson concludes, "What often is misunderstood is that *most churches that close are new churches*"; indeed *"over half* of closed churches come from new churches."[75]

Despite anecdotal judgments of past church development survival rates ranging from 5 to 65 percent, many denominations are now claiming success as high as 90 percent.[76] As recently

73   Olson, *The State of the American Church*, Slide 129.
74   Ibid., Slide 78. "Some groups count a new church the instant someone begins working on it (in which case many start and close all in one year); others only count them when they are fully rooted. The above figure takes this into account, reporting on the net results of new church planting. Having been started and rooted though, many of these still may close within the first ten years."
75   Ibid., Slide 79 italics mine. "For example, in the Southern Baptist Convention, churches started before 1980 had a yearly closure rate of 0.6 percent (6 closures per 1000 churches); churches started after 1980 saw three times the rate of church closure—1.7 percent. Another example is the United Methodist Church. Very few UMC churches close—they have a rate of 0.18 percent churches closing each year (1.8 closures per 1000 churches), one-fifth that of the Southern Baptists. Yet their closure rate for churches over ten years old is 0.08 percent, less than half of the whole group's rate."
76   Southwestern Assemblies of God University, "Program in Church

as 1999, Paul Becker and Mark Williams cited denominational groups with *mortality* rates as high as 70 percent.[77] If Olson is right that half of the churches that close each year are "new churches" (defined by Olson as churches ten years old or younger), and we are closing three thousand churches each year, then roughly 1,500 of these are *new* churches or failed church "plants." What is the real number? All that can be said with any degree of confidence is that somewhere between 30 and 70 percent—or approximately half—of all attempts to establish new congregations result in churches that survive ten years or longer. The Becker/Williams numbers compared with Olson's data can be interpreted to demonstrate an improvement in new church survival rates. If this is the case, the improvement is likely due to an increased reliance on new-church pastor assessment and on boot camps or church-planter intensives conducted by denominations to help prepare leaders for real-world field conditions.

How do we interpret these data? I read the data as positive news in at least two ways. First, it appears that more than half of the churches are surviving. This is better than the rate for new entrepreneurial start-up businesses and reflects a profound improvement over past numbers. Second, it appears that we have a great deal of control over the success or failure of the new churches we start. If we "execute on the basics," implementing what might be called "church parenting best practices," our future efforts will almost certainly be more successful than our past ones have been. Another positive interpretation of these

---

Planting and Revitalization Now Offered," Southwestern Assemblies of God University, http://70.86.83.194/news/article.php?page Num_news=10&totalRows_news=342&ID=13 (accessed December 2, 2006). For example: "In statistics recently published on the A/G website, churches planted using a proven and intentional system have a 90 percent survival rate after 5 years, while Assemblies of God churches that do not, have only a 50 percent survival rate."

77   Paul Becker and Mark Williams, *The Dynamic Daughter Church Planting Handbook*, ed. Jim Carpenter (Oceanside, CA: Dynamic Daughter Church Planting International, 1999), 96.

numbers: they are much higher than the anecdotal evidence or the word on the street and urban myths of church planting would seem to indicate. My guess is that most of my readers will be surprised that the success rates for new-church efforts are much higher than they imagined. My hope is that this revelation will prove motivating for some—maybe for you. Why not try a holy experiment? Chances are the result will be a life-changing Christian community, impacting people for the cause of Christ, transforming a community for the Kingdom of Heaven.

Mother Church Story—Early Mistakes Corrected

Background

Joe Wittwer has served as senior pastor of Life Center in Spokane, Washington, a church with Sunday attendance of over 5,000 people. Over the course of six years, Life Center parented four new churches, each within a seven-mile radius of the mother church, each sent out with seed congregations of between 200 and 800 people, and each with staff leadership teams as large as five full-time members. I interviewed Pastor Wittwer at Life Center in March of 2007. Here are his words:

Interview Excerpts: Joe Wittwer

In the mid 1990s we were doing three services and they were all full. We were thinking, "We could spin off a church, one a year—send out a couple hundred people. That would open up a couple hundred seats that we could take the next year to fill up." Our second thought came from a book about franchising. The reason franchises work is that an entrepreneur gives you the standard operating procedures, you reproduce it, and it will succeed. McDonald's comes in, does a survey, and puts in the golden arches. You go in: same menu, same service. Well, the way churches were being planted wasn't that. It was like sending a couple out who rent a storefront, hang up a shingle that says, "Burgers," and start flipping. What if we sent out churches and, from the first day they opened their doors, people walked in and said, "Hey, this is just like Life Center."

We prayed real hard and the Lord sent us a guy. We put him on our staff and his only job was to gather a church out of our church. We told him, "You've got an unlimited fishing license, you can ask anyone," and he did! He asked our best givers, he asked staff members, our council members. The positive thing is that, after thirteen months, we launched a great church. It was a huge success, and that church is still doing well today.

On the negative side, number one: the pregnancy was way too long. By the time he got close to the end, people were more than ready for it to be done. The second thing was that the unlimited fishing license wasn't a good idea. It created a lot of emotional tension. Let's say you're the worship leader and you see this guy talking to your top worship guy. They might be talking about the Mariners, but you assume he's recruiting your best guy. The third thing was that we didn't give him a role to be part of our church, to absorb our DNA. He had this huge core from Life Center who said, "We don't feel like we are a daughter church; we feel like a divorcee." It was our mistake not his, but he was defining himself by how he was going to be different from Life Center.

Round two came up two years later. The second church planter led our kids' ministry for two years. It was a six-month instead of a thirteen-month gestation. I did the fishing instead of him. I would have him preach and then I would get up and say, "This guy is going to plant a church. Most of you are going to stay here. But some of you are going to feel a tug from God. If you feel the tug, go."

He did a brilliant thing. He got his core from Life Center all thinking about their lost friends—built evangelism into the DNA of this new church. On their opening Sunday, they had a couple hundred people from Life Center, but they had a couple hundred people, or more, from the surrounding community. These changes made the second one a lot more fun. They are a church of 1,200 now, doing four services.

Some surprises. First big surprise: The first church we sent out, four hundred people go out the door. Twenty-five percent of our income walked out the door in one Sunday. That Sunday they left, our attendance was only down by forty! Over the next nine months, we made budget every month. The second church plant, two hundred went out. That same Sunday, our attendance was up two hundred! As fast as we sent them out, the seats filled back up again. The second big surprise was who went. We thought, *The people who will go are the people on the fringes.* Instead, half of our worship team went, half of our drama team went, half of our church council went. Three members from our staff went. Now the good news was that we had a whole new level of leadership that came up. I think about one small group I did with several couples—this is my small group—and half of them left and went with a church plant. They drive past our church, and go ten more miles to this new church!

In March of 2002, Curt, who is one of our top staff leaders, came to me with tears in his eyes and says, "I think God is calling me to plant a church in the valley." I was stunned. For five years he said, "I'll never plant. This is home." We already had a church plant launching—and we were trying to raise ten million dollars! Long story short: as soon as Brad launched in September, Curt started his ramp-up. We finished our campaign and, three weeks later, Curt launched, starting out with 785 people.

[This parent-church effort] is honestly one of the things I am genuinely and appropriately proud of. It is really important to keep people, but at some point the church has got to become a sending group, too. I think every church ought to parent. We want to reach ten percent of our county by the year 2020. By 2020, there will be about a half million people in the county, so we would like to see 50,000 people worshiping in churches that we have planted. We see ourselves multiplying and planting as many churches—different kinds of churches in different ways and sizes and shapes—all across the community. I would love to get to the end of my run, whenever I get to hang up my spurs, to look back and see that we have met that goal.

CHAPTER 3
THRIVING CHURCHES: NO OTHER GOAL

The planting of yet more churches which damage their most committed members, and further alienate those already beyond the reach of existing churches, will hinder rather than advancing God's mission.[78]

—Stuart Murray

Consider the sea turtle. According to the children's picture book, *Life Cycle of a Sea Turtle*, "Out of every 5,000 eggs, *only one* will end up as an adult sea turtle."[79] After the mother sea turtle lays the eggs deep in the sand, she leaves. Forty-five to seventy days later, the hatchlings "swim" up through the sand, taking three days to reach the surface, then they begin the journey to the ocean.[80] With shells still soft, the newly hatched reptiles make a tasty snack for wild dogs, pigs, sea birds, crabs, raccoons, insects, and even people.[81] Having reached the ocean, they face still more fierce predators. Of the 100–150 eggs laid by the average mother sea turtle, how many will reach adulthood?

---

78 Murray, *Church Planting*, 159.
79 Bobbie Kalman, *The Life Cycle of a Sea Turtle*, The Life Cycle Series (New York: Crabtree, 2002), 13 italics mine.
80 Ibid., 16.
81 Ibid., 15, 18.

The answer is zero. Fifty mothers must each lay 100 eggs for one sea turtle to survive! Why? "A mother sea turtle does not look after her eggs."[82] Here is the technique: "After the mother sea turtle finishes laying her eggs, she covers them with the sand that she dug up. She throws more loose sand around the nest and presses it down with her body. The sea turtle's job is now finished, and she heads back to the ocean."[83]

Now consider the gorilla. Another children's picture book, *Little Gorillas*, begins with the question, "What animal spends its day in the forest being cuddled, rocked, and pampered?"[84] The answer, of course, is the baby gorilla. If the young sea turtle's early life is the epitome of neglect, the gorilla's is the ideal example of nurture and care. Instead of one hundred each year, the mother gorilla has only one baby every four to five years. Her life is transformed by birthing and raising the baby. She nurses it for two years and sleeps with it for three. She carries it everywhere. Once the baby is strong enough, it climbs on her back and rides there, usually not beginning to walk on its own until after its second birthday. And, she does not nurture her little one alone. "All the gorillas in a family visit a new baby. They all want to touch and kiss it. The mother gorilla, however, holds the baby closely to protect it from the noisy activity."[85] Even the fierce, giant silverback, the dominant fighter of the gorilla clan, nurtures the offspring. If the mother dies, her orphaned infant may often be seen clinging to the bright silver fur of the backs of the strong family leaders.[86]

I am not the first to compare various strategies for starting new churches with different parenting styles from the animal kingdom. David Olson uses the terms "reptilian" and

---

82 Ibid., 16.
83 Ibid., 14.
84 Bernadette Costa-Prades, *Little Gorillas* (Milwaukee, WI: Gareth Stevens, 2005), 3.
85 Ibid., 4.
86 Ibid., 9.

"mammalian" to describe approaches of various denominations and groups:

> Reptilian church planting systems follow their namesakes—they plant large numbers, but leave them to make it on their own, causing lower survival rates. Mammalian church planting systems follow their namesakes—they plant smaller numbers, but make sure as many as possible survive to healthy adulthood.[87]

One denominational district supervisor is rumored to have made a habit of sending young pastors off to start churches with the words, "Here's $10,000. If you're anointed, you'll make it; if not, we won't have wasted much money." The philosophy is to start a lot of churches with little investment. A few will survive and thrive. After the others fail, we can pick up the pieces and gather them back into our churches. This is *sea turtle* church planting.

There is a serious downside to this approach: the people. The people who lead these churches feel used and disheartened. The people who are part of these churches feel as if God has failed them. The communities in which these attempts are made end up immunized against further attempts to start new churches. More often than not, the outcome is neither clear success nor clear failure, but something in between. The results are communities of between twenty-five and seventy-five people with no visible presence in the community, unable to purchase a building, participate significantly in mission efforts, or support full-time staff. A few congregations rise above this level, but the majority struggle along for years until they finally give up and the church folds.

Not long ago, my church staff and I read Steve Sjogren's the *Perfectly Imperfect Church* as an ongoing group devotional.

---

87   Olson, *The State of the American Church*, Slide 88.

I was horrified to read, in his description of four kinds of churches, these statements about the "struggling church":

- The goal is to survive from week to week.
- Constant effort is required just to keep things afloat.
- One family leaving creates a crisis.
- It's scary and unpleasant for all.
- After a while struggling churches can become *toxic for all involved.*
- *We actually become emotionally sick* from a church situation that drains us, with no end in sight.
- Involvement for a prolonged period of time is *unhealthy at every level for everyone involved.*[88]

As we read this together, I realized that this was exactly where I lived. I had pioneered a church, it had peaked at 120 people, and, due to my allowing too much change all at once, the church declined to about eighty-five. Sjogren was describing my church. Every month I was scared we would not meet budget. One day after our 6:30 a.m. Tuesday Men's Group meeting, one of the guys told me he had something he needed to talk to me about. "It's nothing big," he said. We took a walk around the block, and he revealed his "nothing big" announcement was that he and his family would be leaving the church. Nothing big!? This was a model family—they tithed, she served in children's ministry, and they had three beautiful children, a strong marriage, and a vibrant faith. They were an excellent match for the community we were trying to reach. They were exactly the kind of family we needed. I affirmed Ryan in his spiritual process, prayed with him, thanked him for the time they had given to the church, blessed him, said good-bye, and ran to God with angry, desperate tears inwardly shouting, "I

---

88 Steve Sjogren, *The Perfectly Imperfect Church: Redefining the "Ideal" Church* (Loveland, CO: Group, 2002), 20–21, italics mine.

thought you called me to plant this church. Are you with me in this, or not?" After five years, the ministry began to feel very much like Sjogren's description. We had tried everything, but we had no resources and we were tired.

A couple of years ago, a local church pioneer pastor for whom I have great respect stepped out of ministry when his doctor put him on disability. The energy and dedication he had invested in his church had been Herculean. He had a world-class Web site, a polished media- and technology-savvy worship service, and church members leading virtually every city and community event. His congregation of 150 had more presence in our community than the local five-thousand-member mega-church. A vibrant church, but too much of it was on the founding pastor's shoulders.

Why do I tell stories like this in a book ostensibly written to motivate the multiplication of new churches? My hope is to create a new paradigm: to do away with sea turtle church planting and replace it with gorilla (not to be confused with *guerilla*) church parenting. If we do this well, perhaps we can create a culture in which the vast majority of our new church efforts will do more than simply survive, they will thrive.

"Thrive" Defined

The goal of every church parenting effort should be birthing a thriving church. A thriving church is different from a mega-church. It is important to begin with this statement. Sjogren describes what he calls the "pretty good church" or the "perfectly imperfect church."[89] As pastor of a church of six thousand, he believes a church can be too *big* as well as too small. Some of the characteristics of Sjogren's ideal church are: (1) "average total weekend attendance of three to five hundred," (2) "large enough to enjoy the strength of a varied staff," and (3)

---

89   Ibid., 23–26.

"large enough to [birth][90] a new church now and then." Sjogren goes on to enumerate thirteen adjectives describing his vision of the perfectly imperfect church: simple, upward, outward, anointed, fun, safe, inclusive, trusting, atmospheric, generous, true, cooperative, and leading out.[91] Thriving is about more than numbers, but it is at least *partly* about numbers. Sjogren asserts there is a minimum numerical threshold a church must reach in order to be healthy, alive, and life giving. I agree with him. A thriving church does not have to be huge, but there is a line below which a congregation will fail to experience a sense that they are thriving. Perhaps that number is three hundred to five hundred; maybe a little smaller if the church is young.

Church health author and consultant Christian Schwarz enumerates eight quality characteristics he believes will unlock the latent natural growth potential in any church:[92] empowering leadership, gift-oriented ministry, passionate spirituality, functional structures, inspiring worship services, holistic small groups, need-oriented evangelism, and loving relationships.[93] Again, thriving is about more than numbers, but Schwarz demonstrates convincingly that congregational health and numerical growth usually go together.[94] Both weekly attendance and numerical attendance growth are part of what it means to thrive—especially when a church is young.

With these thoughts in mind, I propose six distinct characteristics of a thriving young church. As we consider

---

90 I am trying to rid the church-multiplication world of the term "plant."

91 Sjogren, *The Perfectly Imperfect Church*, 26. Some of these are self-explanatory; some are not. For those that are not, I recommend Sjogren's book.

92 Christian A. Schwarz, *Natural Church Development: A Guide to Eight Essential Qualities of Healthy Churches*, 4th ed. (St. Charles, IL: ChurchSmart, 2000), 14. "Natural church development does not attempt to 'make' church growth, but to release the **growth automatisms** [bold original], with which God Himself builds the church."

93 Ibid., 22–37.

94 Ibid., 20–21.

parenting and nurturing new churches, it is helpful to keep in mind a focused image of what we want to bring into being. Here are six distinct characteristics of a thriving young church:

T—Transforming communities
H—Healthy leaders—in pairs
R—Reproductive vitality
I—Instant momentum
V—Visible presence
E—Enough resources

T: Transforming Communities

When I set out to plant Hillside Chapel, someone asked me, "Why do you want to plant a church?" Or, put another way: "What will this new work bring to the target community that will set it apart from other churches already there?" These questions were embarrassingly difficult to answer! On the day our core was sent out from the mother church, our district supervisor justified starting another church. He said, "It will create another context in which the gospel will be preached." This is an important criterion, but perhaps not the decisive one.

I prefer the way New York City church pioneer and movement leader Tim Keller lived out the answer to this important question:

> Tim Keller came to New York in 1989 with a clear, compelling purpose: to apply the gospel to New York City so as to change it spiritually, socially, culturally and, through it, to change our society and the world … He wanted to see the gospel applied in such a way that it would transform the city.[95]

---

95   Keller and Thompson, *Church Planter Manual*, 24. © Used by permission.

Keller does more than leave this city transformation mission in general terms. His vision is profound, clearly defined, and specific. Here it is at length:

1.   Change in the overall level of civility: *Drastically reduced crime*, drastically *reduced levels of corruption*, integrity in dealings and interactions, greatly increased neighborliness.

2.   Change in family structure: *More families* staying and settling in, better relations between the sexes. *"Ex-gay" a proven and respected path*, yet active homosexuals not bashed. More marriages healthy ones, yet single life not scorned or stigmatized.

3.   Change in race and class relationships: *Great reduction of racial tensions*, and innumerable cooperative efforts between the "haves" and indigenous leadership among the "have-nots." Literally *hundreds of community development projects*.

4.   Changes in cultural work being produced: Art, scholarship, literature, theater, movies, foundations for the arts producing work that is *inspired by special revelation of Christ* or at least by the general revelation of the Creator and the moral law and the dignity of humanity.[96]

Is he starting a church or running for mayor? I'd vote for him! The thousands of people who joined him in this mission have voted with their feet and created a historic modern-day church-multiplication movement that transformed New York and several other American cities. Why? His success results from the clarity of vision to start a church and transform a

---

96   Ibid., italics mine. © Used by permission.

community in a thoroughgoing manner in accordance with gospel values from law enforcement to the arts.

H: Healthy Leaders—in Pairs

The vast majority of new churches are started by one ministry couple. The rationale for this is simple: it is difficult enough to assemble a budget to support one couple, why even try to support two? It turns out there is a good reason to support pairs of leaders. Ed Stetzer, director of church-multiplication for the Southern Baptist Convention's North American Mission Board, conducted some of the most extensive research available on the topic of starting new churches on this continent. He writes:

> One of the recurring themes from the church planter surveys was the need for church planting teams ... There is a demonstrable attendance difference when there is more than one church-planting pastor on staff. The attendance is almost double. It is not just the presence of multiple pastors that makes a difference. *This mean attendance is most present when there are two staff members*—but not three or more. In all cases, more staff is better than a single staff pastor.[97]

Two is the number. Stetzer's research demonstrates the importance of the these staff members focusing their full-time vocational effort on the new work[98] and of providing financially for them in such a way that their spouses also can devote full time to the ministry[99]—no small investment in today's urban and suburban environments.

The ideal church planting team consists of two full-time leadership couples—perhaps a senior pastor and worship leader or a senior pastor and a children's ministries director—both of

---

97 Stetzer, *An Analysis of the Church Planting Process*, 21 italics mine.
98 Ibid., 8–9.
99 Ibid., 8.

whom can focus undistracted attention on the fledgling work, and both of whose spouses can assist them in the effort full time.

The couples also need to live in the community they are trying to reach. Keller tells of his commitment to live in Manhattan when he started Redeemer Presbyterian Church:

> This budget enabled me to ... live in the center of New York, instead of commuting from the suburbs like most Manhattan pastors did. I got sharp criticism from some people ... for assuming Manhattan-level rent expense. They said it was bad stewardship and even hinted that it was arrogant and snobbish to want to live in the center city. But I had learned ... the absolute necessity of living as near to your people as possible.[100]

This two-by-two, full-attention, resident-in-the-city model has biblical precedent. "Calling the Twelve to him, [Jesus] began to send them out two by two" (Mark 6:7). Peter and John preached together in Acts 4, and Paul and Barnabas are sent out together, "While they were worshiping the Lord and fasting, the Holy Spirit said, 'Set apart for me Barnabas and Saul for the work to which I have called them.' So after they had fasted and prayed, they placed their hands on them and sent them off" (Acts 13:2–3). This verse also speaks to the full-time aspect. The Spirit instructs the church to set them apart for the work. This is more than simply an act of imparting ritual holiness; it is a practical freeing from other responsibilities in order to give full attention to the work of the gospel.

In Corinth, Paul made tents to build relationships, but as soon as help arrived he put the tents aside and "devoted himself exclusively to preaching" (Acts 18:5). Perhaps this explains why Paul seems so conflicted when he argues for his right to receive

---

100   Keller and Thompson, *Church Planter Manual*, 11. © Used by permission.

support (1 Cor. 9:1–12). He had been set apart and sent out, but some denied him the support he needed to stay focused on the work. Let us ensure those we send out have the support they need to stay focused on the work.

One reason it is so important to send out teams to start churches is psychological. One by one, gospel work is lonely and laborious; two by two, it is invigorating and rewarding. Camaraderie is everything. According to Stetzer's numbers, a church-start team consisting of two full-time ministers and their spouses located in the city in which they are ministering should be many times more effective than the typical lone, bi-vocational pioneer with an employed spouse. If we want thriving churches, we will adopt this model.

R: Reproductive Vitality

> In the darkness, something was happening at last. A voice had begun to sing. It was very far away ... Sometimes it seemed to come from all directions at once. Sometimes he almost thought it was coming out of the earth beneath them. Its lower notes were deep enough to be the voice of the earth herself. There were no words. There was hardly even a tune. But it was, beyond comparison, the most beautiful noise he had ever heard. It was so beautiful he could hardly bear it ... Then two wonders happened at the same moment. One was that the voice was suddenly joined by other voices; more voices than you could possibly count. They were in harmony with it, but far higher up the scale: cold, tingly, silvery voices. The second wonder was that the blackness overhead, all at once, was blazing with stars.[101]

---

101   C. S. Lewis, *The Magician's Nephew* (New York: HarperCollins, 1994), 106–107. © Used by permission.

Do you recognize this scene? It sounds like Genesis, but it's not—at least not *our* Genesis.

> The lion was pacing to and fro about that empty land and singing his new song. It was softer and more lilting than the song by which he had called up the stars and the sun; a gentle, rippling music. And as he walked and sang the valley grew green with grass. It spread out from the Lion like a pool.[102]

Now do you recognize it? This is the creation scene in C.S. Lewis' *The Magician's Nephew*, one of seven books in the children's classic series *The Chronicles of Narnia*. The picture Lewis paints of the hyper-fertile, in-the-process-of-creation land of Narnia has remained in my imagination since I first encountered it as a brand-new Christian in my teenage years. Narnia is created in a short span of time as the Lion sings daisies and buttercups, willows and wild roses, rhododendrons and dark firs into existence. Even the iron bar from the lamppost back home springs to life and grows into full-size lamppost in Narnia.

This is reproductive vitality.

How can Lewis' vision of reproductive vitality be realized in a congregation? The most crucial key is the cultivation of seeds. Seeds are young leaders. New congregations and ministries are and should be born with enthusiastic, spiritually passionate, thoroughly discipled, trusted young leaders. New works will spring from empowered young leaders. For some reason, God has made the young ambitious. Young leaders innately crave something to lead. One role of older leaders is to encourage and free, rather than control or stifle, creative energy. Reproductive vitality will be enhanced as senior leaders invest themselves in the lives of young apprentices, creating opportunities and contexts for new young leaders, giving them freedom both to fail

---

102   Ibid., 112. © Used by permission.

and to succeed. A tension between excellence and opportunity exists in every ministry. Churches with reproductive vitality will err on the side of opportunity, while inspiring excellence through far-sighted, patient modeling and coaching.

Darrell Guder, in *The Missional Church*, emphasizes two additional indispensable practices for the cultivation of reproductive vitality:

> The purpose of leadership is to form and equip a people who *demonstrate* and *announce* the purpose and direction of God through Jesus Christ ... These ministries of leadership are given to enable the church to carry out its fundamental missiological purpose in the world: to *announce* and *demonstrate* the new creation in Jesus Christ.[103]

Demonstrate and announce; announce and demonstrate. Passionate and regular preaching on reproduction is essential. Hands-on demonstration of missional ministry is motivational.

Church-multiplication movement leader and author Ralph Moore asks, "What is the fruit of an apple tree?" The intuitive answer is, of course, an apple. Some might expand to a crop of apples. Others might even say the fruit of an apple tree is an apple tree. Moore's answer: an *orchard*.[104] By analogy, the fruit of a church ought to be more than simply converts; it should be congregations—plural. Healthy organisms not only reproduce themselves, they reproduce *beyond* themselves.

Orchards result from a long-term process. Only at the appropriate time in the apple tree's life cycle will it begin to bear

---

103   Darrell L. Guder and Lois Barrett, *Missional Church: A Vision for the Sending of the Church in North America*, The Gospel and Our Culture Series (Grand Rapids, MI: William B. Eerdmans, 1998), 183–185 italics mine.

104   Ralph Moore, *Starting a New Church: The Church Planter's Guide to Success* (Ventura, CA: Regal, 2002), 255.

fruit. Several years pass before tart green and red spheres drop from limbs. Once mature, the trees will produce only in season. An orchard requires a lifetime's work. But the orchard happens only when, early in the process, the conditions for reproduction are ensured. In the church world this means the cultivation and empowerment of young leaders in an environment of ministry opportunity, reproductive proclamation, and missional modeling. In practice, the order is different: proclaim, model, engage.

Take a moment to reflect with me on the outline of the book of Matthew. After the introductory material in the first four chapters (genealogy, birth narrative, baptism, temptation, and calling of disciples) comes the Sermon on the Mount (chapters five, six, and seven). This is *proclamation*. Jesus teaches Kingdom of Heaven principles to inspire his audience to participate fully in it. Chapters 8 and 9 contain eleven short vignettes wherein Jesus demonstrates hands-on, in real life, the Kingdom of Heaven principles he has taught them earlier. This is *modeling*. The section ends with Jesus' instruction to the disciples to pray for harvest workers. Where do those workers come from? It turns out that the disciples are the answers to their own prayers! Chapter 10 begins, "Jesus called his twelve disciples and gave them authority" and then continues with Jesus coaching his disciples in the methods of Kingdom of Heaven ministry. This is *engagement*.

The three characteristics of reproductive vitality—proclaim, model, engage—must be instilled intentionally in the culture of every new church from its moment of conception.

I: Instant Momentum

My wife Treesa and I have had a long and vibrant tradition of hosting New Year's Eve parties in our home. We always end the night by devoting the last hour of the year to prayer: prayers of thanksgiving for the blessings of the passing year, and prayers that lift up each other's concerns and cares for the coming year.

Last year, we had seventy-five people in our home. One friend left the party saying, "Now that was church!" One year, though, we announced a party and sent out invitations a little late, and nobody came ... except one family. When we greeted them at the door, it was quite awkward informing them that our vibrant party had become a quiet evening with a few close friends.

This same disappointment and discomfort can occur when visitors come to a new church. When we first started Hillside Chapel, I asked all our volunteers to park behind the building so there would be plenty of space for visitors to park. A month later, I changed the plan. Potential visitors had been sighted turning around and leaving because it looked like nobody was there! They had come for a party, but, from the look of the parking lot, all they were going to experience was a quiet morning with a few friends—friends they had never met! When visitors come to experience a new church, it is important that it be *church*, not a small group. Critical mass is crucial. The feeling that they have arrived at a party, a celebration, a real church, is what will draw them back again.

Church growth literature attempts to address the various growth barriers churches face: the one-hundred barrier ... the two-hundred barrier. Many churches never clear these hurdles. Instant momentum can mean a new church can clear these hurdles on the day of its birth. This, of course, requires a launch strategy based on church-multiplication "best practices," intensive pre-launch work by a team of committed staff and volunteers, broad and generous outside support, a well-conceived and well-executed publicity effort, and a strong birth service with a variety of ministries already in place. This will not happen without a high level of commitment from a generous, giving, participating mother church and without a high level of involvement, coaching, tutoring, and mentoring from the sending senior pastor.

V: Visible Presence

Imagine you found just the car you wanted on an Internet auto sales site. The banner reads: "Championship Motors specializes in high-performance automobiles and high-performance customer service." Just what you want. You call the dealer and ask where the lot is so you can see the car. "Well, sir, we don't actually have a lot. Can I just meet you at Starbucks with the car?"

Fifteen years ago, my family and I were looking for a new church. We found a promising ad in the yellow pages and called the number to inquire. A teenager picked up the phone, "Yea?" I asked if I had the right number. "Hold on, I'll go find my dad." Five minutes later, since no one had returned to the phone, I hung up. The church may have had Sunday morning services, but they did not take their ministry seriously enough to have anyone actually answer the phone. What is the definition of a "fly-by-night operation"? It means an organization that is present one day and gone the next—too much like a typical new church that meets in a rented school building!

A new church needs a home. Ideally, the church will have an adequately equipped office in a visible place staffed by someone other than the pastor who will answer the phone and create a professional presence when people call. A reception area, a waiting space, and a private pastor's office with a door are the minimum required for safe, ethical operation of a church. It is better if a meeting space adequate for small gatherings can be included as well. This assumes the church is meeting in rented space on Sunday mornings, as do almost all new church starts. The best situation is to create a way for the new church to have its own place, including an excellent worship space, twenty-four hours a day, seven days a week. The combination of an excellent Web site, a welcoming voice on the phone, and a physical presence in the community will help a new church win the trust of people in the community as a legitimate organization, serious about meeting the needs of the community. The level of provision needed for a dedicated meeting space like this may seem impossible, and, in many situations, it may indeed be impossible. That is why the final characteristic in the "THRIVE" acronym is so important.

E: Enough Resources

If you are considering becoming a mother church, you might feel somewhat overwhelmed by the amount of resources obviously required to provide a staff, a strategy, and a location for a baby church. You are right to feel that way. Imagine how the young pastor of a fledgling congregation must feel facing the lack of these ministry essentials.

Fortunately, there are several potential funding sources for a new work, so the mother church should not have to carry the full burden. Most denominations will assist financially. Other churches in the denomination might pitch in. Members of the new congregation will likely tithe (usually at a higher percentage than in an established church). Pioneer pastors should always raise some support from their own sources. If pastors cannot ask others for money, they will probably also have trouble asking for important faith commitments of other kinds. There are independent non-profits dedicated to church-multiplication that may help fund new works. Some denominations have foundations dedicated to evangelistic efforts.

Regardless of the source of the money, every effort should be made to ensure that adequate funding exists, both for ministry basics and for community outreach and impact events. Assuring adequate funding is a role of the mother-church pastor. It is likely that the mother-church pastor is more experienced and better connected within denominational and ecclesiastical structures. The organizational savvy and relational network of the mother-church pastor can make a huge difference in the efforts of the young pioneer pastor to garner the support needed to free the baby church so it can begin to grow up. A good analogy is missionary funding. A potential missionary is usually required to establish a clear budget, including a realistic amount for personal and family support. They will then begin a process of fundraising that may occupy the span of a year or more. They enter the mission field only after they have procured donations and pledges sufficient to cover both initial moving expenses and annual support. Those funds will come from a wide range of donors, both large and small. In the same way, a pastor going out to start a new church should not rely on a single source of funding: the mother church alone. Instead, multiple sources of funding should be combined so that the new work will not be choked by financial need too early. If a pioneer pastor is not sufficiently patient or bold to gather funding from multiple donors, they likely also lack the nerve and perseverance required to succeed in leading the establishment of a thriving new church. A pastor representing Tim Keller's movement arrived in our town a few years ago with almost $250,000 in the church account—gathered via an extended time of pre-launch fundraising. This was before he had a single church member! Imagine the resilience that can be instilled in a new congregation if this kind of responsible missionary-style, multi-source funding is ensured.

Mother Church Story—Thriving New Congregations

Background

Pastors Jon and Cindy Burgess pioneered New Hope Seattle in 2005 in Shoreline, a suburb north of Seattle. They now have two services every Sunday, a building of their own, and weekly attendance of about two hundred. They are venturing out to birth their first daughter congregation by establishing Matt and Stephanie Leon in ministry on Capitol Hill, a rapidly changing, trendy, urban neighborhood adjacent to downtown Seattle. I interviewed Jon and Cindy in the offices of New Hope Seattle. Here are their words:

Interview Excerpts: Pastors
Jon and Cindy Burgess

Interviewer: Tell me the story about how this seed of an idea of birthing a new church came about and how you became convinced this was something that God would have you do.

Jon: We felt, when God laid Seattle on our hearts, that the way to reverse the statistic of its being one of the most unchurched cities, having one of the highest suicide rates, was not to build some megalopolis church. What if, instead, we were to start churches that would reach people groups resident right here?

We started talking with our team, "We're going to be planting more. Some of you may be church planters." Of course, that freaked them out. It freaked us out even as we were saying it!

Cindy: We had it in our hearts that New Hope Seattle would be a birthing center: a place where we reproduce churches—and the churches we birth can birth churches.

Jon: We were thinking, "Five years in, we'll be mature enough to birth another one." Then you, the troublemaker, had a church-parenting conference. I took two young leaders. We weren't even two years old, averaging one hundred a Sunday, and moving into a building. You put the map on the wall and asked, "If resources weren't an issue, where would God lead your heart to plant?" The two guys next to me, August and Matt, both said, "Capitol Hill."

Right after that, Jim Hayford said, "There is this pizza place my friend Danny owns on Capitol Hill and he wants not only to open it up to start a church, but he'll pay you to be there." I looked at August and Matt. They looked at me. I said, "Fill out that sticky note and stick it on that wall."

Cindy: You know what's funny? At that same time, we found out we were pregnant. It was a total surprise. We had two boys and weren't planning on having more and … we got pregnant.

Jon: I asked August and Matt to pray with their loved ones. Matt and his wife Stephanie felt this was the thing God had designed them for all their lives.

Cindy: Stephanie had never wanted any involvement in ministry.

Jon: She was nice about it, but inside was thinking, *No way.* Then, as she came before the Lord honestly, she realized, "This is already where God has me." Our church has been working with a youth drop-in center downtown. Stephanie had been there on Friday nights ministering to prostitutes.

I asked them to pray, "You know who is in this church and you know Capitol Hill, so you know some people would be a great fit, and some would not do well. Pray who you might want to approach and say, 'Would you be interested in being on our team?'"

Cindy: They are meeting Mondays with six to eight leaders, going through books together. They are going to start a meditation service where people can read Bibles and listen to music and have a contemplative time.

Jon: After the book time, Danny Piecora is setting up a band and coffee house night—Christian and secular bands. The team is going to be there to hang out and build relationships, to create a safe place to ask questions—a forum for spiritual discussions. They are meeting both the main languages on that hill: music—there are clubs all over the hill—as well as the intellectual longing to discuss and to look at all the angles.

Jon: It would be a mistake to take what works for Shoreline and make it fit on Capitol Hill.

Cindy: At first I was thinking, *If we're New Hope, we have to do it like New Hope.* Value-wise it will be the same; style-wise, the dressing is going to look different.

Jon: The church that sent us to Seattle is New Hope Kapa'a, Kaua'i, Hawai'i. When the congregation heard the vision for New Hope Seattle, this two-hundred-member church said, "We are going to support you." They paid our rent and utilities so I could devote my time to building a team and meeting people. Even though they are across the ocean, they are our mother church.

New Hope Seattle looks different from our Parent-church in the Islands, but the spirit is the same. People come from island churches and say, "Hey, it feels like home here." We have the same DNA. The DNA of our sons is similar to ours, but our sons are not exactly like us. Even though they express it differently on Capitol Hill, the DNA is going to be the same. They are going into that place knowing, "We get to be comfortable in our own skin."

Because Cindy and I weren't from the area, we didn't know anybody. Three local pastors helped us get a solid footing. That is the other thing I like about the church parenting model: it is not just one church that is responsible for the success of a new church; it is everyone in the area creating a womb effect.

We are sending our best leaders. Our best intercessors are going. Two of our worship leaders are going. Our hospitality leader is going. You give your best to your kids. You want them to grow up strong and healthy. You'll make sure they have food before you have food, that they have clothes before you have clothes.

I meet with them every week, talking through difficulties they are running into. One of the scariest things for a church planter is when they feel like, "I am getting lost in the shuffle here. I don't even remember why I am doing this." I keep bringing them back to, "Let's keep this really natural. God's calling you to this. Look at the team that he's building. Look at the relationships in the community." They'll bring something up and say, "I'm sorry. This doesn't really have to do with church planting." I say, "This has everything to do with it.

As you develop a solid relationship with each other and with your team, that's going to make for a solid foundation for this church." The church parenting model encourages the idea that the core of everything is relationship. It is as natural as nursing a child.

CHAPTER 4
NEW CONGREGATIONS FOR
EMERGING GENERATIONS

The loss of tens of thousands of people from British churches throughout the 1990s, for instance, was related less to where these churches met than to the kinds of communities they were and the kinds of subculture they represented. Planting more and more churches of the same kind will not reverse this trend.[105]

—*Stuart Murray*

At a 2001 national denominational convention in Jacksonville, Florida, church-multiplication leader Jared Roth offered a memorable challenge. As a mantra to guide our efforts, Roth gave us three words: young, east, cities.[106] He challenged the idea that a pioneer pastor must be forty years old and hold multiple degrees to succeed in starting a new church. "Raise your hand if you were a senior pastor in your twenties," he prompted the 2,000 pastors assembled there. I was struck by the response. Almost every pastor over fifty-five years old stood with hand in

---

105 Murray, *Church Planting*, 129.
106 "East" is a denominational priority, and I will leave "cities" to authors emphasizing urban evangelism.

the air; hardly any below that age did. Our movement had clearly undergone a change. In the early years of booming expansion and evangelistic zeal, we were not slow to send a young pastor right out of Bible school out to start a new work. As we have matured, those zealous young twentysomethings have come to look younger and younger. Now it is hard to take the idea of a senior pastor in his or twenties seriously. Instead, we want to see five to ten years as a youth pastor and an advanced seminary degree. The giant and gigantically influential Willow Creek Community Church had its first service on October 12, 1975.[107] Founding pastor Bill Hybels was born in 1952.[108] If my math and my sources are correct, Pastor Hybels was twenty-three years old that day. Other than an honorary doctorate from his alma mater, he still does not have any advanced degrees. World famous author and mega church pastor Rick Warren was born in 1954.[109] Under his leadership, Saddleback Valley Community Church held its first service on Easter of 1980.[110] Warren was just twenty-six years old! The deployment of young pioneer pastors to start churches among emerging generations must be one of our highest priorities in the parenting of new churches. Notice two emphases in that last sentence: *young pastors* and *young congregations*. There is only one way to get a young congregation: start a church in a community in which young people live.

A few years ago, a young pastor approached me about birthing a new church. At twenty-four years old, he had a four-

107   Willow Creek Community Church, "History—Willow Creek Community Church," Willow Creek Community Church, http://www.willowcreek.org/history.asp (accessed May 10, 2007).

108   Laura Kaczorowski, "Willow Creek Community Church," University of Virginia, http://religiousmovements.lib.virginia.edu/nrms/willow.html (accessed September 3, 2007).

109   Biblio.com, "Rick Warren Biography," Biblio.com, http://www.biblio.com/authors/623/Rick_Warren_Biography.html (accessed September 3, 2007).

110   Saddleback Church, "The Saddleback Story," Saddleback Church, http://www.saddleback.com/flash/story.asp (accessed September 3, 2007).

year Bible degree, a few years' youth ministry experience, an entrepreneurial gift, a proven evangelistic track record, and a small core of devoted disciples—he was an excellent candidate. He was proposing, however, to start a church in a wealthy, established northeast suburb of Seattle where an average house cost three-quarters of a million dollars. The couples who lived there were typically highly educated, well-established in their careers, and, if there were children in their homes at all anymore, they were typically teenagers about to leave for college. People like this were not going to choose this very young—and even younger looking—pastor as their spiritual leader. Besides, they were at a stage in life where they had already made their spiritual commitments. If they were going to go to church, they had a church. If they were not going to church, a zealous, young twenty-four-year-old was not going to have the maturity or wisdom to coach them through the difficult spiritual questions of post mid life.

Here is the question I asked him: "If you were to buy a home, where would it be?" This is a key question. The most fertile combination is a young, passionate, evangelistically oriented pastor in a community where young families are buying their first homes and starting families. This can happen in two ways: Where are affordable, starter homes being constructed? Where are prices in older existing neighborhoods turning around so that young couples can afford to buy homes there? This young man answered, "We've been looking at homes in Monroe. We can buy a home there for $200,000." I said, "Take your team to Monroe and pray together about a new church there." They launched a church to reach the youngest adults moving into this outer-edge-of-suburbia, fast-developing bedroom community.

The reason for this emphasis on new congregations for new generations is twofold. First, whether we call them "bridgers" (born 1977–1994), "millennials" (born 1977–1994),[111] "mosaics" (born 1984–2002), or "the rising generation" (born 1992–2005)

---

111   Stetzer, *Planting New Churches*, 105.

there is a marked vacuum of Christian faith and practice among North America's youngest adult populations. Second, young adulthood is an especially fertile life stage in terms of evangelistic receptivity, second only to adolescence—one in which the establishment of new congregations has proved to be an especially powerful tool.

Missing Faith Commitment

The present emerging generation of young adults in North America demonstrates a lower degree of Christian faith commitment, church attendance, and participation in spiritual practices than in any other living generation. This conclusion is verified by several excellent and reliable studies undertaken by scholars from a wide variety of faith perspectives. In an interpretive article based on his *State of the Church 2006* study,[112] conservative researcher George Barna concludes:

> Twentysomethings continue to be the most spiritually independent and resistant age group in America. Most of them pull away from participation and engagement in Christian churches ... In fact, the most potent data regarding disengagement is that a majority of twentysomethings—61 percent of today's young adults—had been churched at one point during their teen years but they are now spiritually disengaged.[113]

According to Barna, those "bridgers" who were raised in the Christian faith are moving away from the churches established by and for their parents. Comparing the "wide and possibly

---

112　Barna, *The State of the Church: 2006.* © Used by permission.
113　George Barna, "Most Twentysomethings Put Christianity on the Shelf Following Spiritually Active Teen Years," http://www.barna.org/barna-update/article/16-teensnext-gen/147-most-twentysomethings-put-christianity-on-the-shelf-following-spiritually-active-teen-years (accessed March 19, 2010).

growing swath of secularism among Americans" to previous trends in Canada, the United Kingdom, and other Western democratic societies,[114] the *American Religious Identification Survey 2001* (ARIS) notes a clear trend toward non-participation in religious practice among young adults:

> The greatest increase ... has been among those adults who do not subscribe to any religious identification; their number has more than doubled from 14.3 million in 1990 to 29.4 million in 2001; their proportion has grown from just eight percent of the total in 1990 to over fourteen percent in 2001 ... The proportion of the population that can be classified as Christian has declined from eighty-six in 1990 to seventy-seven percent in 2001.[115]

The ARIS report showed more quantitative growth by far in one religious identification category than in any other: the category "no religion." Over 6.5 million people switched into this category; only 1.1 million switched out! From which demographic group does this growing secularity come? Those aged between eighteen and thirty-four at the time of the study, roughly equivalent to the bridger generation, far outpaced all other categories in professing a secular or "somewhat secular" outlook.[116] Categories showing noteworthy growth for the eighteen-to-twenty-nine age group between the 1990 and 2001 ARIS reports include Muslim/Islamic, Buddhist, Mormon, and, more encouragingly from an evangelical perspective, Assemblies of God.[117] Young adults are experimenting with alternative religions—or with a syncretistic mix of spiritualities—rather than continuing in their parents' evangelical faith.

---

114   Kosmin, Mayer, and Keysar, *American Religious Identification Survey 2001*, 6.
115   Ibid., 10–11.
116   Ibid., 21.
117   Ibid., 32–33.

There is sustained evidence of a significant difference in faith commitment from generation to generation. In response to the statement, "Your religious faith is very important in your life," 10 percent more respondents indicated strong agreement in each succeeding generation: "five out of ten mosaics, six out of ten busters, seven out of ten boomers, and eight out of ten elders."[118] Similar results apply to the statements, "The single most important purpose of your life is to love God with all your heart, mind, strength, and soul;"[119] and "You are completely committed to personally making the world and other people's lives better."[120] Age, generation, and stage of life also made a big difference in the Barna study's measure of active faith, "ranging from just 11 percent among mosaics to 28 percent among busters, 33 percent among boomers, 41 percent among builders, and 49 percent among seniors."[121] Levels of self-perceived commitment among those describing themselves as Christian have risen markedly over the last ten years: from 44 percent to 54 percent.[122] Barna also notes a decline in *self-identifying* Christians in emerging generations. He writes, "Among the more interesting patterns is that of the mosaic generation ... There has been considerable fluctuation in their perceptions, suggesting that perhaps they are a generation not

---

118 Barna, *The State of the Church: 2006*, 20. Barna uses the term "busters" to denote the demographic age group that follows the "boomers." As *boomer* relates to the large quantity of babies born in the wake of World War II, *buster* relates to the relatively small number of births in the decades immediately following. The term also connotes the relative dearth of career opportunity available to this age category post-college.

119 Ibid., 24.

120 Ibid., 26.

121 Ibid., 48. A person was seen to have active faith if they responded affirmatively to all three of the following questions: "In the last seven days, did you read from the Bible, not including when you were at a church or synagogue? In the last seven days, did you attend a church service, not including a special event such as a wedding or funeral? In the last seven days, did you pray to God?"

122 Ibid., 12.

overly comfortable with the label 'Christian' but not ready to abandon the faith that they are most comfortable aligning with."[123]

Perhaps Barna's data may be interpreted to indicate not a generalized decline in Christian faith among emerging generations, but a stage of development in adolescence and early adulthood in which every generation becomes less comfortable identifying themselves with Christianity.[124] It appears, however, that the situation is more serious than this. The Barna team concludes:

> One of the most frightening trend lines is that of the mosaics, the youngest adults in the nation. Traditionally, young adults are the least likely to demonstrate much zest in their spiritual life. However, the gap between the beliefs and behavior of this generation and the figures representing the four older generations does give reason to pause and pray ... mosaics are substantially less likely than baby busters—the next youngest generation, and a group that itself is generally below average on most spiritual indicators—to reflect a commitment to Christianity. For instance, mosaics are 36 percent less likely than busters to say they are absolutely committed to the Christian faith; 18 percent less likely to describe their religious faith as very important to them; 24 percent less likely to have made a personal commitment to Christ; 61 percent less likely to have an "active faith," 24 percent less likely to read the Bible and 21 percent less likely to pray to God during a typical week. They are also less likely to hold an orthodox view of God, to accept the Bible as totally accurate in the principles it teaches; to accept the

---

123   Barna, *The State of the Church: 2006*, 8. © Used by permission.
124   Ibid., 14. "Not surprisingly, the younger a person is, the less orthodox their view of God tends to be."

existence of Satan; to reject the idea that Jesus sinned; and are less likely to be born again.[125]

One factor that makes the need to communicate the gospel to the Mosaic generation especially acute is their parents' spiritual disengagement. They are not learning the Christian faith in their families of origin:

> Until three decades ago parents of young children were typically among the most devoted to spiritual regimens, hoping to raise their children with good spiritual habits and perspectives. Today, there is little distinction between the parents of youngsters and adults who do not have such a responsibility. Given the significant influence of one's family on the shaping of a person's faith life, and the fact that such influence is most dominant prior to the young person reaching age thirteen, this pattern showing the absence of parents as spiritual guerillas is unnerving.[126]

The online publication *Canadian Social Trends* reinforces the notion that, as young adults, this group, having lacked spiritual leadership and nurturance in their formative years, presently demonstrates much less spiritual interest and involvement than any other generational group. "In 2004 over half of Canadians aged fifteen to twenty-nine … either had no religious affiliation or did not attend any religious services."[127] This is not an isolated conclusion: "Consistent with previous studies, young adults are the group with the weakest attachment to organized religion. However, even when other forms of religious behaviour are considered, almost half of Canadians aged fifteen to twenty-nine still have a low degree of religiosity."[128]

125   Ibid., 52. © Used by permission.
126   Ibid., 53. © Used by permission.
127   Crompton et al, *Canadian Social Trends 2006*, 2.
128   Ibid., 7.

This self-perception of high spiritual commitment without a corresponding congregational involvement or devotion to spiritual practices is especially marked among the mosaic/bridger/millennial generations. Mosaics were among those who perceived *themselves* to be most committed to the power of faith community as a transforming and maturing influence.[129] It is alarming, and perhaps a bit perplexing to note that 58 percent of mosaics have "never attended a Christian church service, other than for a holiday service ... or for special events."[130] The younger a person is, the less frequently he or she prays,[131] serves,[132] and reads the Bible.[133]

To summarize all this, North American young adults are:

1. moving away from the historic faith of their parents,
2. generally uncomfortable calling themselves "Christian,"
3. attending church far less regularly than any other living generation,
4. believing themselves to be spiritual without engaging in any spiritual practices or religious disciplines,
5. much more frequently aligning themselves with non-Christian or pseudo-Christian religious organizations,
6. increasingly secular in orientation, and
7. receiving less spiritual nurturance from their parents than previous generations.

---

129   Ibid., 27. Twenty-five percent strongly agreed with the statement, "You cannot become a complete and mature person unless you belong to a community of faith that influences you," in contrast to 18 percent of the general population.
130   Ibid., 36.
131   Ibid., 40.
132   Ibid., 39.
133   Ibid., 34.

Barna concludes: *"If these patterns remain stable for a number of years, they spell trouble for the Christian church."*[134]

Evangelistic Receptivity

There is a surprising paradox among these emerging young adults: their very disengagement from faith makes them ripe for the gospel—if proclaimed in their language. James R. Engel, discussing receptivity in unreached people groups, delineates two primary factors that indicate increased openness to the Gospel: 1) seeking or open to change, and 2) low level of existing religious commitment.[135] Both of these characteristics are especially true of those in the early stages of adult life in the United States and Canada:

In 1990, Donald McGavran advised, "Reach out to persons in transition. These are much more likely to be receptive than during periods of relative stability."[136] Among the significant life transitions he identifies are "first job," "getting married," and "first child"—all young-adult rites of passage. In assessing the spiritual openness of a city for the purpose of church-multiplication, the very first question Ralph Neighbor suggests we ask is: "How many children live there?"[137] Pointing to

---

134   Ibid., 12 italics mine. The study continues: "It is also worth noting that the commitment levels measured among boomers have climbed considerably in the past decade. In 1996, just 43 percent of 'Christian' boomers were absolutely committed to Christianity. Since that same year, the increased commitment among busters has been even greater, rocketing from 27 percent to the current 42 percent."

135   James R. Engel, "Using Research Strategically in Urban Ministry," in *Planting and Growing Urban Churches: From Dream to Reality*, ed. Harvie M. Conn (Grand Rapids, MI: Baker, 1997), 49.

136   Donald A. McGavran, *Understanding Church Growth*, rev. ed. (Grand Rapids, MI: William B. Eerdmans, 1980), 259.

137   Ralph W. Neighbour, Jr., "How to Create an Urban Strategy," in *Planting and Growing Urban Churches: From Dream to Reality*, ed. Harvie M. Conn (Grand Rapids, MI: Baker, 1997), 113.

what he calls "the young developing suburb," characterized by young adults buying homes and having children, Neighbor charges, "Target these areas ... for they contain some of the most responsive segments of the city."[138]

New Congregations for Emerging Generations

Regardless of faith, today's young adults generally do not like attending *traditional* worship services, where their numbers are down. And they shy away from labels, increasingly identifying with no specific religion or, if they are Christian, calling themselves non-denominational. *Yet in conversations and in academic surveys, generations X and Y still demonstrate an overwhelming belief in God and an interest in how all things spiritual relate to their lives and the world around them.*[139]

One reason young adults, as open and spiritually responsive as they are, are not in church is this: they need churches of their own—*new congregations for new generations.* An article in the *South Florida Sun-Sentinel* concludes, "Rather than moving away from religion, today's young adults are moving toward God—on their own terms ... Many do not see religion as a tradition to cut and paste from one generation to the next."[140]

David Anderson, pastor of the large and growing Bridgeway Community Church in Columbia, Maryland, and a leading proponent of multi-cultural ministry, drives home the point that young Americans see existing churches as irrelevant: "Some 40 percent of Americans age eighteen and younger are non-Anglo ... and they perceive churches as archaic—the more unicultural the church, the more archaic."[141] John Holzmann

---

138   Ibid., 116.
139   Jamie Malernee, "The Gospel of Youth: 20-Somethings Shy Away from That Old-Time Religion," *South Florida Sun-Sentinel*, September 25, 2005.
140   Ibid.
141   Barnes and Lowry, "Special Report: The American Church in Crisis," 103.

articulates six "missiological presuppositions" that inform his efforts to provide research to help others reach cities by starting new churches. At least three of these speak to the question at hand here:

1. "It is by local congregations—churches—and not merely individuals that God intends to fulfill his purpose of discipling the nations. To establish *indigenous* churches is a missiologically strategic goal."[142] If we are to reach young adults, we must establish new churches *for* them—and they must be indigenous *to* them.

2. "God desires that every people have the opportunity to worship and serve him within a church that reflects their unique cultural and social structures, as sanctified by God."[143] The cultural differences between generations on our continent are greater than we imagine. New congregations for new generations must incorporate what is distinctly theirs from a socio-cultural point of view.

3. "A major barrier to the gospel's advance among many unreached peoples is the perception that Christianity and the church are 'foreign.'"[144] *Boomer* and *builder* generation churches are foreign to *bridger* generation young adults.

Most writers use statistics and conclusions regarding the bridger generation to motivate efforts to reach *youth*—high school and middle school students. Born 1977–1994, the youngest of the bridgers are still in high school, but *the eldest of the bridgers are presently over thirty-years-old!* Certainly

---

142   John Holzmann, "Caleb Project Research Expeditions," in *Planting and Growing Urban Churches: From Dream to Reality*, ed. Harvie M. Conn (Grand Rapids, MI: Baker, 1997), 53–54. © Used by permission.
143   Ibid.
144   Ibid.

many to most of them have entered their careers, married, and begun having children of their own. The bridgers are now young adults! The way to reach them now, in their newly acquired adult status, is through the parenting of new congregations for emerging generations. The strategies and techniques that interested them and touched their lives as adolescents will no longer reach them as they mature. What was accomplished in the teenager by Christian concerts featuring alternative bands will best be done in the emerging adult through the establishment of new congregations.

Regardless of generational labels, the formation of new congregations has historically been—and continues to be—the best way to reach emerging generations and disciple them in the Christian life. Veteran church growth researchers Dudley and Roozen conclude, "New congregations are much more likely to attract young families with children in their homes than are older, more established congregations."[145] The converse is also true: one of the best ways to birth impactful churches is to attract and evangelize young adults, especially those with young children in their homes,[146] gathering them into new congregations, indigenized and acculturated to young-adult ways of being and thinking.[147] This was true of the Jesus Movement churches of the 1960s and 1970s, exemplified by the Calvary Chapel group centered in Costa Mesa, California. It was true of the Seeker-Driven movements of the 1980s and

---

145   Dudley and Roozen, *Faith Communities Today*, 13.
146   C. Kirk Hadaway, "Learning from Urban Church Research," in *Planting and Growing Urban Churches: From Dream to Reality*, ed. Harvie M. Conn (Grand Rapids: Baker Books, 1997), 41. "Growth or decline . . . results from changes in and characteristics of the context. Population growth or decline is the most important factor [including] *the proportion of young children in the area*" italics mine.
147   Of course, it is possible to cite situations in which successful new churches are established that are not targeted toward emerging generations: in geographical areas of rapid development, during stages of initial evangelism of a people group, in growing concentrations of ethnic peoples, or in burgeoning retirement communities.

1990s, epitomized by Willow Creek Community Church in South Barrington, Illinois. It is proving true in the Emerging (or "Emergent") Church movement in this new millennium, characterized by authors such as Brian McLaren (*A New Kind of Christian*[148] and *A Generous Orthodoxy*[149]), Mike Yaconelli (*Stories of Emergence*[150]), and Donald Miller (*Blue Like Jazz*[151])—and embodied in such churches as Mars Hill Bible Church, pastored by Rob Bell (*Velvet Elvis*[152]), and Mosaic, led by Erwin Raphael McManus. The timeless phrase *semper reformanda*—ever reforming—conveys the truth that the church must reinvent itself for every emerging generation, and that these new generations, as they embrace the gospel, must organize themselves into autonomous congregations. The gospel is unchanging; the cultural forms within which the gospel expresses itself, however, must be ever changing.

This phenomenon is not unique to this set of three generations; it will always be true that the churches belonging to the parents' culture will need to remake or replace themselves in order to reach the children's culture. *New congregations for new generations* is an abiding principle. It applies to the bridger, buster, millenial, post-modern, and mosaic generations—and it will apply to the next generation, and to the one after that.

---

148   Brian D. McLaren, *A New Kind of Christian: A Tale of Two Friends on a Spiritual Journey* (San Francisco: Jossey-Bass, 2001).
149   Brian D. McLaren, *A Generous Orthodoxy* (Grand Rapids, MI: Zondervan, 2004).
150   Mike Yaconelli, *Stories of Emergence: Moving from Absolute to Authentic* (Grand Rapids, MI: Zondervan, 2003).
151   Donald Miller, *Blue Like Jazz: Nonreligious Thoughts on Christian Spirituality* (Nashville, TN: Thomas Nelson, 2003).
152   Rob Bell, *Velvet Elvis: Repainting the Christian Faith* (Grand Rapids, MI: Zondervan, 2005).

Mother Church Story—Emerging Generations Reached

Background

Pastors Serena and Rob Wastman recently led the establishment of a new congregation in the Alki Point area of West Seattle. The birth of "Journey of Faith" was the result of a community youth outreach called "Skate Church," which Serena and Rob founded and led, being taken into the womb of their surrogate mother church, Westside Foursquare, under the leadership of Pastor Dan Johnson. I interviewed Serena Wastman at a local coffee shop and Dan Johnson in his West Seattle home. Here are their words—first Serena's and then Dan's:

Interview Excerpts: Serena Wastman

Interviewer: Tell me the story about how God inspired you and led you to birth this new congregation.

Serena: First of all, without question, Westside Foursquare is the right church to be our parent. We were having a service three weeks ago. It was just wonderful, and Pastor Dan Johnson was there. I slid up to Dan and said, "Isn't this incredible to see a church being born?" She's beautiful and she's lovely and God created her.

Rob and I were youth pastoring in West Seattle. Three years ago, the Lord started to move in us. We were in this tiny church in this little conservative community. Kids started loving one another and loving God. The youth group started growing, and it got bigger than the church. The church was having trouble. The pastor quit, membership went down, and the denomination took over the church. We said, "What should we do with all these teenagers?" They said, "Find some other place and take them with you." Dan Johnson said, "Your youth group can come here." Dealing with teenagers is like opening the doors to a tornado. They'll punch holes in the walls and mess up the carpet. Before we moved to Westside, I told him, "I think God's calling us to start our own church, maybe more than one." What kind of church would take us in: this messy bunch of teenagers that feel called to start something new? They messed the place up and that church body loved us. I have to admire Dan. He welcomed those kids in.

We moved over to Westside with just our leadership team. We offered to help the other church. We said again, "Just love those kids." Sure enough, kids follow where they're loved, so kids started following us over there. When God called us to start this church, we determined that we again would just take our leadership team. When we did plant, all sixty kids stayed at Westside, because they are loved there. We are starting anew in West Seattle with new kids ... kids who have never heard about Christ. From the minute we landed at Westside, it was temporary. They were like our surrogate mother because we were already pregnant.

Interviewer: When you talk about your leadership team, who are you talking about?

Serena: They used to be youth, but the funny thing about youth: they grow up! Now half of them are college age. We're a quirky band of people that have been together for three to five years. I think that's what makes us unique: this church is what college-aged youth would create. It somehow resonates with the culture we're in. I mentioned the word *bohemian*. It's totally bohemian. You have to kick off your shoes and sit on the floor!

One of the drafts was: "What if we just throw in with Westside and set a marker: when Westside grows to *x* number, then we plant Journey of Faith." As we entertained that concept, we could see that it was not going to work. The two styles don't match for long term. Our church plant guy kept saying, "Set a date and launch." So we did. It's obvious how to plan a program when you set a date and back everything up. It's like having a baby. Once you know the due date, you know you've got to get the nursery set up. Setting a date was a real faith walk. "You mean everything God called us to do is going to become a reality?" Before that point it was all ethereal. Our team is so pumped. They got out of the boat and they didn't drown.

We have done great youth services, so doing a launch was not a problem. We did draft services up until March 4. Everything went wrong. We had to keep saying, "Did God call us to this? Yes. We're going to do it, and the sound system's blowing and people are sick." The Sunday before March 4, the lights blew, the sound system went out, and we just worshipped anyway.

March 4 was like a great homecoming—people we loved, people who had been part of our lives, neighbors, family. It was a heartwarming experience. Mentors were there, pastors who had led us to the Lord were there. I was choked up the whole time. Isn't that like the birth of a child? The sound system was fine. The worship team was nervous because they're a bunch of kids, but they're passionate about God. I kept saying, "Just close your eyes and pretend like you're all alone worshipping God."

We are totally pumped that everything God has called us to do is happening. As part of our vision, we wanted to open a store right in the business sector of West Seattle. Retail space is expensive in West Seattle: eight thousand dollars a month. We're a little church; we can't afford that! Two weeks after we launched, we got this phone call from this senior center where we meet on Sundays. "We've got retail space right on the street out front." They would rent it to us for a thousand a month. Churches tell these stories and I always think, "Why doesn't that ever happen to us?" So here it happened to us. "We'll take it!"

In a lot of church offices, you have to ring a buzzer to get in. You can't get in! The lost are trying to get into the kingdom, but you gotta ring the buzzer! Our thought was: if we ever had a church office, we'd leave the doors open and we'd want it right in the middle of the world, the community. So we opened this storefront and, as we were painting and getting it ready to open, the lost and the broken were coming in—and they were distracting us. "Can't you see I've got to paint the walls?" The world needs Christ and they were coming in the doors and we couldn't even paint the walls. It took us six weeks to get that storefront done because we would drop the paint rollers and sit and pray with people.

It's a hang-out center. We sell pop and ice cream—and we sell skateboards, because we're reaching out to youth—and we've got couches and guitars, and people are jamming. We are called to broken-hearted people—not the people who have been rotating churches. There are great churches in West Seattle and we are pointing people as fast as we can to great churches, but the broken-hearted are dwelling with us.

Interview Excerpts: Dan Johnson

Interviewer: Tell me the story about the time that you led your church to birth a new congregation.

Dan: I'll never forget my lunch with Jared Roth, probably the last week I was living in Bend, Oregon, in preparation of moving here. Jared said to me, "Promise me one thing: that someday you'll plant a church on Alki Point [in West Seattle]." As administrator of the district, his whole heart was to plant churches. I said, "I would love to do that." I had a certain paradigm where I had to demonstrate I had grown the church a certain amount to justify being able to plant a church. We've done fine financially, but it's been a missions-focused church. We have started many churches in Romania and we've got quite a few dollars going out for missions so, realistically, my paradigm was I'd need to be a larger church to be able to plant a church. I'd need the personnel and hadn't had anybody step forward that I saw as a church planter. There were several things that kept me thinking we weren't ready.

It was probably two years ago that Rob and Serena Wastman came to us. And it was a ready-made plan. They already had the vision in their heart for the same thing Jared had said twelve years earlier: to start a church on Alki. I was very happy to support them and grace them and let them come in. We provided a platform for them, for Rob and Serena, but also all of their youth. We blended our youth group with their youth group and allowed their youth to take on worship leading and speaking and teaching. I allowed Rob and Serena several times on Sunday mornings to teach and to speak. We invited Serena to sit in on our staff meetings. The influx of their youth and their gifts reenergized and gave new life and vitality to our church without compromising the integrity of our identity. It was an exciting time, and the additional meetings and the additional hassles were all worth it—we birthed a new church out of our church!

We launched the first Sunday night in March. We had a fair number of pastors and twenty-five or thirty people from our own church there. They probably had two hundred twenty people that first night. Since then, they have probably run thirty-five to forty-five. It is still primarily youth. Over the months that they've met from March, April, May—now we're at the end of May—there have been about twenty-five to thirty salvations.

Interviewer: What did Westside do as a congregation—as a mother church—to participate as you sent out the Skate Church to start?

Dan: We made a decision to support them financially—five-hundred dollars a month—and we have had several people in our fellowship go over there. My youth leader has been there several times playing bass. My volunteer children's pastor and her husband have gotten to know Rob and Serena really well. They have been there quite often to support them—just by their presence. We have sent out a number of people, but they're still tied into our church too. Last summer, I met with some of their young men on Thursday nights for a number of weeks in terms of further discipleship.

In the first couple of months, I had weekly contact with Serena. It hasn't been quite every week. Whenever she needs something or needs to talk, I am there to talk. Rob came by about a week ago. I have continued to provide counsel and encouragement. I sense that they appreciate being able to come to me.

It was a great thing for people to see us reach out to embrace new people coming in and, at the same time, being free to release them. It encouraged the whole church to understand that part of why we're here is to release people into ministry and develop their gifts. It was great for our church knowing that we were a part of something larger than us: that we could birth a new church and that it was an extension of our ministry, that we would have a vital part of that and a continuing vital relationship. Over the next four Wednesday nights, our youth group will be meeting with the Alki Skate Church, the youth group from Journey of Faith, along with a youth group from the Baptist church at Lincoln Park—nice weather and a fun time together, maybe some worship and maybe some outreach.

Even though it was a surrogate mother situation, it still had all the elements: the transitions, their coming in and then leaving, costing us financially, sending people out—and we've seen God send us a couple of college-aged guys who are helping us now with the youth. God will send us new people as we are liberal with giving away people, developing them for ministry. This process has challenged me to, all the more, release people and let people make mistakes.

Interviewer: How do you feel that the birthing of this new church has impacted the health and vitality and attendance patterns of the parent church?

Dan: Most years our attendance has ranged between eighty-five and ninety-five on Sunday mornings. There were times where it would be over a hundred. With Rob and Serena coming in and then leaving, there are a few more people, but attendance is not measurably higher. When they came, they were more involved Wednesday nights, so we didn't see a big Sunday morning bubble.

We did see that God blessed us financially. In December, when we made the decision to support them, our tithe had been about twelve to thirteen thousand a month. We had stretched a year ago to believe for fifteen thousand and we really weren't making that. In December, we had a large month, probably twenty-four thousand in tithe income. Extraordinary! When Rob and Serena came to us, we were finishing up a parking lot project and had just increased our mortgage. Through the first four months of this year, we have been averaging between fifteen and sixteen thousand a month. We had one month where it was nineteen thousand.

When Jim Hayford became district supervisor of the Seattle District he said, "My vision is for every church to plant a church. When you birth a church, God will bless your congregation." We have seen that financially, and I believe we are seeing that people-wise, too.

CHAPTER 5
LEAVING A LEGACY: BRINGING MEANING TO LIFE

The key to the fire within is our need to leave a legacy. It
transforms other needs into capacities for contribution.
Food, money, health, education, and love become resources
to reach out and help fill the unmet needs of others.[153]
—*Stephen Covey*

Legacy is a complex concept to define. The Web site Dictionary. com describes legacy as "anything handed down from the past, as from an ancestor or predecessor." This is an accurate definition, but not a comprehensive one. The term finds its etymology from the legal system (notice the common root) as it applies to wills and inheritance. Historically, legacy referred to properties and possessions approved by a legate to be passed from one generation to another after a death, but the term has taken on philosophical and sociological subtlety. It no longer refers primarily to property and goods; it now suggests character and the essence of personhood as embodied in what we have

153   Stephen R. Covey, A. Roger Merrill, and Rebecca R. Merrill, *First Things First: To Live, to Love, to Learn, to Leave a Legacy* (New York: Simon and Schuster, 1994), 49, emphasis original.

done. Our legacy is that by which we will be remembered. It is what we contribute to the world that will last beyond our years. In *First Things First*, Stephen Covey explores the deeper aspects of legacy:

> The need to leave a legacy is our spiritual need to have a sense of meaning, purpose, personal congruence, and contribution. ... To compartmentalize or even ignore the spiritual dimension of life powerfully affects each of the other dimensions. It is meaning and purpose that give context and fulfillment in all other dimensions.[154]

Healthy individuals possess a desire to leave something positive to the world. Perhaps this is why so much of our life satisfaction is bound up in the welfare and character of our children. Ultimately, our children are what we contribute to the world that lasts beyond our years. The satisfaction of legacy requires more than simply leaving something to the world; it means a contribution that is intrinsically deeply meaningful and impactful. Covey frames legacy in the tension between the compass and the clock and ties it to deep personal concepts such as conscience principles and values:

> Our struggle to put first things first can be characterized by the contrast between two powerful tools that direct us: the clock and the compass. The clock represents our commitments, appointments, schedules, goals, activities—what we do with, and how we manage our time. The compass represents our vision, values, principles, mission, conscience, direction—what we feel is important and how we lead our lives.[155]

---

154   Ibid., 45–48.
155   Ibid., 19.

My interest in leaving a legacy through parenting new churches resides deeply in Covey's compass—although it certainly has required a great number of clock hours! In 2003, I had the privilege of participating in a guided process of spiritual exploration, which, among other things, included the articulation of personal values. The fifth of seven values I identified is:

I have a desire to leave a legacy, making my life count for the good of humanity and for the expansion of God's Kingdomon earth. I will invest the gifts and talents God has placed in me for the purpose of blessing and benefiting as many people as I possibly can. I will found organizations, write books, and submit articles. I will speak, teach, lead, and mentor for the purpose of pointing people to Jesus and encouraging them to follow him with all of their hearts. I will touch the untouchables and bring the gospel to the most needy. I will allow myself to dream God-sized dreams. Then I will pray fervently and work diligently to see those dreams fulfilled. I will not allow fear or feelings of insignificance to intimidate me or block me from accomplishing all that God would have me do.[156]

---

156   Here are my seven values: 1) I passionately pursue a personal relationship with God; 2) I treasure my wife and children and want to see them become all God has made them to be; 3) I deeply enjoy the aesthetic pleasure derived both from God's majestically beautiful creation and from contemplation of the transcendent mystery of God himself; 4) I have a passion to read and absorb the best of human thought and to know and understand all my intellect can grasp about God and what he has made; 5) I have a desire to leave a legacy, making my life count for the good of humanity and for the expansion of God's Kingdomon earth; 6) I have an inexplicable and almost un-suppressible inner compulsion toward balance and order; 7) I enjoy the freedom of being alone and independent, but I recognize the need to make this enjoyment subservient to other values that have much greater intrinsic worth.

A fulfilling legacy is something to be pursued with energy and passion. It will not come to us if we sit back and wait.

The Bible on Legacy

Legacy is biblical. The second commandment demonstrates God's multi-generational, historical perspective:

> You shall not make for yourself an image in the form of anything in heaven above or on the earth beneath or in the waters below. You shall not bow down to them or worship them; for I, the Lord your God, am a jealous God, punishing the children for the sin of the parents to the third and fourth generation of those who hate me, *but showing love to a thousand generations of those who love me and keep my commandments.* (Exod. 20:4–6 TNIV)

I have encountered Christians who lay an unhealthy focus on "generational curses," focusing on the punitive aspect of God's proclamation. Notice, however, that any remnant of curse fades within a few generations. God's generational *blessings*, however, last a thousand generations. Even using the most conservative definition possible, a thousand generations is twenty thousand years! God desires to bless and give life—and he desires to do so through a multi-generational perspective, to pass the blessing on from one generation to the next. Even the name of the nation Israel demonstrates God's focus on legacy as embodied in generations. All the progeny of the feisty, wrestling individual whose name God changed to "Israel" go by that name—even to this day.

God also made—and still is in the process of fulfilling—a multi-generational promise to David. When David desired to build a house for the Lord, Nathan initially made the mistake of affirming him in this agenda. After praying, however, the courageous prophet said:

The Lord declares to you that the Lord himself will establish a house for you: When your days are over and you rest with your ancestors, I will raise up your offspring to succeed you, who will come from your own body, and I will establish his kingdom. He is the one who will build a house for my name, and I will establish the throne of his Kingdomforever. I will be his father, and he will be my son ... Your house and your Kingdomwill endure forever before me; your throne will be established forever. (2 Sam. 7:11b–16)

God does not see David simply as an individual. He sees David ultimately in terms of the Messiah who will be the culmination of the generations of David. It is through Jesus that ultimately God's promise to David will be fulfilled, not only in the construction of an earthly temple, but in the fulfillment of all the temple means and does. Peter articulates this multi-generational vision of God in his messianic interpretation of Psalm 16:

Brothers and sisters, we all know that the patriarch David died and was buried, and his tomb is here to this day. But he was a prophet and knew that God had promised him on oath that he would place one of his descendants on his throne. Seeing what was to come, he spoke of the resurrection of the Messiah, that he was not abandoned to the realm of the dead, nor did his body see decay. God has raised this Jesus to life, and we are all witnesses of the fact. (Acts 2:29–32)

Pastoral Legacy

In conducting interviews of parent-church pastors for this project (edited versions of which appear in this book), I was profoundly surprised by how deeply these pastors consider the parenting of new congregations a part of their personal ministry legacies. This began in a pre-interview conversation with my friend and ministry colleague, Dr. Bruce Norquist, but it also came through in the formal interview I conducted with him later. He said, "This is the most rewarding thing we have ever done, *the most rewarding thing I have ever experienced in ministry* ... I have a warm glow of satisfaction as if somehow I am involved in something really significant and really meaningful. The new church is not unlike ... one of my children. I feel that strongly about this church plant." Pastor Dan Johnson told me, "I believe it is a great legacy to birth a church out of our church. Part of the legacy is giving away people, developing them for ministry."

Pastor Joe Wittwer, who is the chief visionary behind an extensive parent-church movement, reported on an opportunity he had to speak to a ministerial association in the Spokane area:

> I think every church ought to parent. I was just talking to a group of pastors, and I asked them, "How many of you are pastoring a church plant?" About three of them raised their hands. I said, "Three of you got it right. The answer is every one of us. Our churches started somewhere. Here in Spokane, the whole city has only been around one hundred years, so somewhere in the last hundred years, or fifty, or thirty, or twenty, someone had the vision and the courage to plant your church—the church you are pastoring. Maybe it was you, maybe it was six pastors back, or four pastors back, but someone had the courage to plant that church. You wouldn't be doing what you are doing if they hadn't done it." We're

all standing on someone else's shoulders. The question is that legacy thing: What are we leaving for the next generation—the generation ahead?

Stephen Covey presents the ideal of an individual who has integrated the "four human capacities," including that of legacy, into his or her character. He writes, "When we reach a 'critical mass' of integration, we experience spontaneous combustion—an explosion of inner synergy that ignites the fire within and gives vision, passion, and a spirit of adventure to life."[157] This kind of enthusiasm and adventure is embodied in the churches that Wittwer has brought into being from Faith Center.

Legacy of a Congregation

Each of these pastors obviously sees the congregation or congregations he has helped birth as integral to his personal ministry legacy. As important as this is, however, it is not the most important aspect of legacy that can come out of the parenting of new congregations. It is very possible—and quite common—for the senior pastor of a congregation to be involved in the birth of a new church, but for church members to see very little of the process and, therefore, have little or no sense of congregational legacy. Often, the senior pastor of the mother church is the only person in the church that has a strong relationship with the lead pastor who is going to be sent out. This is especially true when the pioneer pastor has come from outside the church, perhaps as a new seminary graduate or as someone recruited from leadership in another church of the same denomination or affiliation. As rewarding as helping a young pastor start a new church can be for a mentor, it is crucial that a sense of legacy and connection be instilled in the congregation as a whole. An average member of the mother church ought to know that a new church is being or has been

---

157   Covey, Merrill, and Merrill, *First Things First*, 48.

born, ought to share in the enthusiasm and excitement of the birth, and ought to have participated in the launch of the new church in some way.

Building a sense of legacy in the parent congregation is a relatively simple task, but it requires intentionality and sustained attention. At the conception stage, when the decision is being made to bring a new church into the world, the decision ought to be made in consultation with the church's official lay leadership bodies. The decision should not be made in isolation as the sole decision of the senior pastor as is often done. If the church has a congregational polity, the members should vote. If the church has a presbyterian polity, the session or elder board should make the decision. In an episcopal or modified episcopal polity the advisory council should be consulted and their ideas taken seriously.

As soon as the decision is made, the project should begin to receive regular and focused public attention. Meet-and-greet luncheons should be held with the leadership team. Every Sunday should include platform-level announcements. Printed materials and informational videos should be produced. Service projects into the targeted community should be organized, and the whole congregation of origin should be invited and encouraged to participate. Sermons should be preached about missional priorities. Church members should be encouraged to pray about becoming part of the core of the new church and should be asked to give sacrificially toward it. This kind of public profile and congregational involvement must continue up until the birth of the new church—and beyond.

When we launched Hillside Chapel, the children's ministry staff and volunteers from Eastside Foursquare Church, one of our two parent churches, devoted a week of their summer to take part in a Vacation Bible School in our target community. Hillside had not yet conducted a public worship service. Eastside Foursquare Church provided decorations, T-shirts, curriculum, staff, enthusiasm, and helped us make a strong positive initial impression. There is no way we could have done it without them. We did not know how to go about running this Bible school, and we did not have the resources, but for them it was a repeat for our thirty kids of what they had done for three hundred the previous week. This involvement was not simply a distraction or inconvenience for these already-overworked staff members, it was part of the process of establishing a sense of legacy in our mother church.

Once the new church has been birthed, it must not disappear from the mother church's radar screen. Regular reports of the new congregation's progress should be given from the pulpit and in written and online communications. Joint community service projects should continue. Volunteers should be sent from the mother church to the new church to fill needs that cannot be met by the fledgling congregation (it should not be expected that volunteers should flow the other way). Anniversary services and joint worship services should be held bringing together mother church and new church. The mother church should continue to give financially out of budget and should encourage individuals within the congregation to give to the new church above and beyond tithe dollars (which must continue to go to the mother church). Ultimately, bringing a new church into being is the congregation's work and ought to involve every congregant at every stage. If this is done, the church will experience a powerful sense of ownership—and ultimately legacy—as the new congregation takes its first steps and becomes a fruitful community-changing force for the Kingdom of Heaven. Floyd Tidsworth asserts, "Inherently, people want to keep their names alive. They want the ideals and characteristics which they hold dear to be perpetuated."[158] This is the sense of legacy that can be shared by every member of a mother church, and by the congregation as a whole.

---

158   Tidsworth, *Life Cycle of a New Congregation*, 100.

The Possibility of a Mixed Legacy

When asked about the possibility of birthing a new church, one potential parent-church pastor told me, "I don't want to birth a new church because I am afraid of passing the dysfunctions of this congregation on to the new one." It is genuinely unavoidable that something like this might happen. A baby church will always include many of the characteristics of its parent(s)—both positive and negative. This idea is analogous to a young couple who might say, "We don't want to bring children into a world as terrible as this one." Though there is much that is evil and dangerous about the world, bringing loved children into the world, who will be taught to reflect Jesus' Kingdom of Heaven ethics in all they do, can do nothing but change it for the better. Of course, they will suffer and experience difficulty—and even do some harm along the way. The world, however, will be an indisputably better place because they are in it. In fact, the best way a Christian couple can change the world for the better is to give birth to and raise godly, Christ-like children.

Of course, a couple with severe marital dysfunction or, correspondingly, a church whose congregation is severely unhealthy, should postpone parenting until these troubles have been addressed. Every couple and every congregation, however, have some growing to do. Normal areas of challenge should not prevent parenting in either case. Otherwise, there would be no babies—and no new churches.

In the same way, a new congregation will experience difficult times—and might even make some harmful mistakes along the way. On balance, a new church will almost always impact the world much more profoundly for good. Perhaps it is a calculated risk for a parent congregation to give birth. There are possible negative outcomes. The new church might not survive. The mother church might experience some financial and attendance challenges. Christian Schwarz writes in his classic handbook *Natural Church Development*:

Hardly anything demonstrates the health of a congregation as much as the willingness—and ability!—to give birth to new congregations. The opposite is true as well. Hardly anything is a more clear indication of illness than structures which by design hinder church-multiplication, or at best permit it as an absolute exception.[159]

Schwarz, who considers growth and multiplicative reproduction a natural outworking of health,[160] continues, "Our study showed a clear positive correlation between the quality index of a church and the number of churches it had planted within the last five years."[161]

Legacy and Faith

Legacy and faith are closely related concepts. To leave a powerful legacy, we must act out of a powerful faith. The classic concise New Testament definition of faith—"Now faith is being sure of what we hope for and certain of what we do not see" (Heb. 11:1)—introduces a tribute to those heroes who have left the church with its most powerful legacy. The only characteristic the people on the ensuing list have in common is that they took action to change their lives and circumstances in radical ways as a response to the prompting of their Creator. They are of both genders. They are of various nationalities. They lived in different eras. They experienced different outcomes: some exceptional prosperity; others unmitigated disaster ("some were sawn in two"). But they all moved because God prompted them. If they had not, they would not have left a significant legacy. Here is a longer definition of faith: A mode

---

159   Schwarz, *Natural Church Development*, 69.
160   Ibid., 68. "Reproduction through multiplication is simply a life principle of all God-created organisms, including the church of Jesus Christ."
161   Ibid., 69.

of being characterized not by shrinking back in stagnating, placating, paralyzing fear, but by engaging with God in a kingdom-of-heaven-embracing, long-range-future-oriented, promise-believing, people-blessing, hope-filled, risk-taking, Holy-Spirit-informed, adventurous journey of life. Whether as a church or as individuals, our legacy to the world will exist in direct proportion to our faith-inspired action on behalf of the Kingdomof God.

Mother-Church Story—A Sense of Legacy

Background

Peter and Gabriella Van Breda serve as senior pastors of Bellevue Foursquare Church—also known as The Gathering Place—a vibrant church with average Sunday adult attendance of about three hundred in Bellevue, Washington. Over the past five years, the Van Bredas have led Bellevue Foursquare in the parenting of three ethnic congregations: (1) Iglesia Rey de Reyes, a Spanish-speaking congregation in Federal Way, Washington, pastored by Juventino (Tino) and Maria Arredondo; (2) The Faith Gathering Place, a Korean fellowship led by Hong-Gi (Rick) Kong and his wife Jean that meets within the Bellevue Foursquare facility; and (3) the emerging Bellevue Hispanic Foursquare Church, pastored by Ramon and Yolanda Telemantes, also still meeting in the mother church building. I interviewed Peter and Gabriella in their offices at The Gathering Place in January 2007.

Interview Excerpts: Dr. Peter Van Breda and Rev. Gabriella Van Breda

Interviewer: Tell me a story about a time—or times—when you led your church to birth a new congregation.

Gabriella: Tino and Maria Arredondo had started a church in Yakima, relocated to Bellevue, and wanted to start another church—and we decided to get behind them. We locked in a facility and started financing them—paying their rent, and some extra. Then we took them through the whole process: our ministry institute, assessment, church planting intensive ... everything. They already had a small following that was meeting in their home, so we met with them and conducted leadership training with them down in Federal Way. A staff pastor went down, we went down, and members of our council went down. We also showed them how to follow through with all the denominational requirements—get a federal tax identification number ... set up their books.

Tino is really a good evangelist. He believes in signs, wonders, miracles, prayers for the sick—and he and Maria visit people. Members of the congregation are bringing new people to church. Their facility is in a pivotal position, right on the corner of two very busy streets. After about three years, they have 100–150 adults in worship on a Sunday.

Interviewer: In what ways did you as parent-church pastors invest yourselves in the conception, gestation, birthing, and nurture of the new church?

Peter: All three churches have been different. The Telemantes wanted to come up from Mexico to plant a church here.

Gabriella: The first thing was identifying that this man who wanted to relocate to the United States, and felt he had a call to do so, was sent by God. Peter has had to spend many hours with the Immigration and Naturalization Service, helping them to get R-1 visas [temporary visas for religious workers].

Peter: This is not something where you just say, "Go for it," then go back to your office.

Gabriella: When you build a relationship with them, out of that, they really begin to trust you. It really comes down to investing your time and communicating with them—loving them. We don't charge rent to the churches we've parented, but there will come a time when that will become part of their independence. I want to be careful that we don't overtax them so they can't make their own salaries.

Interviewer: In what ways did your staff, lay leadership, and congregation invest themselves in the new church?

Gabriella: We had to model the fact that we wanted to do this, the fact that we loved these people, the fact that we believed in them. Our church people were very supportive in coming to their kick-offs, and to their services. We have done our newcomers' dinner and lots of functions all together to help the integration. Our people have absolutely loved it. We have had to teach the staff how to work with cross-cultural challenges: "Why don't they do things the way we do?"

Peter: These men are pastors; you respect them for the call that God has on their lives.

Interviewer: How do you feel the birthing of this new congregation impacted the health, vitality, and attendance patterns of the parent congregation?

Gabriella: Some get really excited about it when they realize [church parenting] is part of how Bellevue Foursquare has grown. There are particular families that support the ethnic churches in everything they do.

Peter: There are also crossovers: people who go back and forth between the churches. Sometimes a few Spanish folk come in the morning and then they'll wait for their own service. Some of our folk, I know, are going to the Spanish service.

Gabriella: We even have staff members that are crossing over.

Peter: We have offices here for [the daughter church pastors] and they use all our equipment, and our staff is regularly in contact with them. When I see one of them in his office, he'll either come sit in my office or I'll go and sit in his office and we'll just chat.

Gabriella: Last summer, when we met for our annual divisional lunch, Tino came. I hadn't seen him for a while—and I noticed he had lost too much weight. Maria was telling me about some of his symptoms and I said to him, "You've got to get to a doctor." He said they had an appointment in a month. I said to him: "I want you to see the doctor *tomorrow*." He had diabetes, so we organized to pay some medical bills through the district. Usually, we see the Arredondos at divisional meetings once a month and I try to travel down there once or twice a year to visit their services.

Peter: There is a lot of telephone contact with them.

Gabriella: Tino is starting churches in Mexico, and has had challenges with the denomination. We are helping him navigate those challenges and introducing him to those who run Foursquare in Mexico—helping them work the network.

Peter: Each congregation, as it grows up in its own ministry, needs less and less of our help. Your kids will always be your kids, but, when they grow up, there's a different relationship.

Gabriella: The goal is to create them as independent entities, completely independent from us.

Peter: "Tie no strings but love," somebody once said. We have had three fabulous, amazing couples. We don't see them as children of ours. I think they are more co-laborers in the field with us. I respect them for what they do for the Kingdom of God. That respect makes a big difference when parenting a church.

Gabriella: When we were appointed to this church, we adopted missionaries who were part of the legacy of the initial church. The commitment was that these people would be kept on the field. Part of the legacy of Bellevue Foursquare Church is the missionaries. I am hoping that part of the legacy of Bellevue Foursquare Church one hundred years down the road will be these ethnic church plants.

Peter: I don't understand why other churches don't make room for ethnic congregations. I wish I had more time, more space. We would love to fit a fourth group in here.

PART TWO:

HOW

CHAPTER 6
KEY CHARACTERISTICS AND PRACTICES OF PARENTING

The best church planting occurs when a sponsor/mother church is actively involved ... On countless occasions, I have sat with church planters who were discouraged because they did not have the support and encouragement of a sponsor or mother church. On the other hand, I have visited with many church planters who had the support of a mother church—and they have shared a sense of enthusiasm and excitement.[162]

—*Ed Stetzer*

Several authors have written excellent how-to manuals designed to assist pioneer pastors step by step in the process of starting a new church. Among the best of these are:

- Ralph Moore's *Starting a New Church:*[163] Informed by a great deal of real-world experience (Ralph Moore is founder of the Hope Chapel movement,

---

162 Stetzer, *Planting New Churches in a Postmodern Age*, 76. © Used by permission.
163 Moore, *Starting a New Church*.

which has taken Hawaii by storm), Moore assumes a "hiving-off" model with parent and child churches in close geographic proximity.

- Aubrey Malphurs' *Planting Growing Churches for the 21st Century*:[164] Despite the agricultural metaphor in the title, Malphurs lays out his guide based on the stages of human reproduction and birth.

- Ed Stetzer's *Planting New Churches in a Postmodern Age*: A research-based and extremely comprehensive work, this relatively recent work has nonetheless been revised and re-released under the title *Planting Missional Churches*.[165] The new edition makes an already excellent work more practical, more up to date, and more attractive to young pioneer pastors.

- Timothy J. Keller and J. Allen Thompson's *Church Planter Manual*:[166] Emerging from the outstanding success of Redeemer Church in New York City and the Presbyterian Church in America (PCA), this spiral bound handbook is remarkable for its comprehensive focus on establishing churches that will transform cities and renew their cultures under Christ.

- Nelson Searcy and Kerrick Thomas's *Launch: Starting a New Church from Scratch*:[167] This recent work presents a down-to-earth, step-by-step instructional layout with a conversational story-teller's tone that makes it not only a very helpful tool for birthing new churches, but an enjoyable read as well.

---

164   Aubrey Malphurs, *Planting Growing Churches for the 21st Century*, 2d ed. (Grand Rapids, MI: Baker, 1998).

165   Edward J. Stetzer, *Planting Missional Churches* (Nashville, TN: Broadman & Holman, 2006).

166   Keller and Thompson, *Church Planter Manual*.

167   Nelson Searcy and Kerrick Thomas, *Launch: Starting a New Church from Scratch* (Ventura, CA: Regal Books, 2007).

Every pastor venturing forth to start a new congregation should be required to read and write papers on all five of these books. Many pioneer pastors go forward without bothering to learn from the successes and mistakes of their predecessors, subjecting their congregations and communities to the same set of avoidable errors. With this much written, the role of the pioneer pastor and the process of launching a new church have been thoroughly discussed.

The role of the mother church pastor and leadership has received much less attention. I have discovered two works that may prove helpful to pastoral and lay leadership in the process of giving birth to new churches:

- Elmer Towns and Douglas Porter's *Churches That Multiply*:[168] Designed as a Bible study of the book of Acts, this book is targeted toward the congregation and lay leadership of an existing church. Towns and Porter are bold enough to assert, "The Bible teaches that Christians are to reproduce Christians and churches are to reproduce churches. *Your church should begin a twelve-week process of studying if it should start a new church.*"[169] I like this straightforwardness! This book will prove especially helpful for conservative, traditional churches with a congregational polity.
- Paul Becker and Mark William's *The Dynamic Daughter Church Planting Handbook*:[170] This is a comprehensive seminar manual designed to facilitate

---

168   Elmer L. Towns and Douglas Porter, *Churches That Multiply: A Bible Study on Church Planting* (Kansas City, MO: Beacon Hill Press, 2003).

169   Ibid., 23 italics mine.

170   Becker and Williams, *The Dynamic Daughter Church Planting Handbook*. The unfortunate conflict of metaphors in the title is indicative of the confusion under which the church-multiplication movement operates.

the multiplication of new churches according to a mother/daughter church model. This is an excellent, highly recommended piece. If you are going to parent a new church, *get this notebook and do what it says.* It is not presently published through traditional channels, but can be ordered through the Dynamic Daughter Church Planting International Web site: www.dcpi.org. Becker and Williams seem to be the only authors who have published a manual expressly for the Parent-churchpastor, so their binder offers exceptional worth to leaders who contemplate the sponsorship of a new church.

In light of these excellent how-to guides, my purpose in this work is not to lay out a step-by-step process. Instead, I hope to provide you, a leader in a potential mother church, with tools to help you engage in the church parenting process with discernment, maturity, and wisdom. I do, however, have some strong views regarding three indispensable process-oriented aspects of the role of the mother church, which I emphasize in the paragraphs that follow.

The significant benefits contributed by a mother church are most pronounced in the vulnerable early years of a new effort. Not surprisingly, new congregations with parent churches report attendance 27–28 percent higher in the first two years than those without.[171] Benefits brought by a nurturing mother church, however, go far beyond numerical gains. The spiritual/ emotional health and well-being of the new-church pastor, the pioneer team, and their families, and the reputation of the gospel in the community are also protected by a watchful mother church. The blessings a mother church can bring to a

---

171 Stetzer, *Planting New Churches in a Postmodern Age,* 77. See chart at the top of page. Percentages are extrapolations based on observation of this chart.

child depend greatly on the level and kind of involvement and support the mother church gives.

I will focus my discussion on those church parenting practices that have been demonstrated statistically to make the most difference in the health and growth of the new church. Though, as previously noted, some mother churches have been accused of playing the role "in name only," in cases where the mother church provides weekly supervision for the planting pastor, releases a core of people, and provides the right kind of financial support, the presence of the mother church becomes critically significant to the success of the new work.

Supervision and Camaraderie

Loneliness is one of the great battles faced by pastors of church start-ups. Many church planters come from roles on a large church staff where they experienced a great deal of camaraderie and team spirit. Because of this, they are often unprepared for the reality of being solo pastors, frequently with no office support and a ministry team made up of volunteers engaged in secular careers. Stetzer relates his experience in this regard: "On countless occasions, I have sat with church planters who were discouraged because they did not have the support and encouragement of a sponsor or mother church. On the other hand, I have visited with many church planters who had the support of a mother church—and they have shared a sense of enthusiasm and excitement."[172]

My own experience as a pioneer pastor verifies Stetzer's report. The greatest shock I experienced was the degree to which I found myself suddenly solo. In my previous role, I'd had a full-time administrative assistant working alongside me in ministry. If I needed to pull together a meeting, I would send an e-mail saying, "I need to meet with [insert six names here]. Could you find a time when we can all get together?"

172   Ibid.

By the next day it would be done. If I needed new binders for a membership class, I called our staff graphic artist and said, "Can you update that binder for me? Here's some new text. I want a nautical theme this time." A week later, twenty-five beautiful new binders sat on my desk with five table leaders ready for training and a room reserved with tables and chairs exactly where I wanted them.

As a pioneer solo pastor, if I wanted to have a membership class, I had to write all the copy, do the graphic design, go to the office supply store to buy binders and dividers, take the masters to the copy store, run my personal credit card through the copy machine scanner myself, figure out somewhere to have the meeting, find some tables and chairs, and personally call any volunteers I needed to help set it up. What used to take two or three phone calls in a relational atmosphere of fellowship and camaraderie now took a week's personal task-focused effort.

Probably due to the lower salaries, smaller congregations, and the reduced prestige given to start-up pastors in the early years, the majority are also first-time senior pastors. It is hard to recruit proven, experienced pastors under these circumstances. For this reason, most pioneer pastors have yet to learn many of many of the basic lessons of church leadership. Nonetheless, it is typical to send them out to either succeed or fail on their own with infrequent supervisory meetings at best. The solution to both these problems—loneliness and inexperience—is the same: weekly supervision. Statistically, *weekly* meetings for the purpose of supervision of the new-church pastor result in a *near doubling of attendance* figures in each of the first four years *when compared even to monthly meetings.*[173] Stetzer attributes this greater success to greater levels of accountability. While this may be true, greater success could also be related to the impartation of insight and the greater levels of camaraderie,

---

173   Ibid., 93 italics mine. See chart "Frequency of Meeting Supervisor." Based on attendance numbers, monthly supervisory meetings are statistically no better than a total lack of supervision.

teamwork, and personal and institutional support that are a likely companion to weekly supervisory meetings. Very surprisingly, frequency of supervisory meetings appears to affect church plant attendance numbers as much or more than any other single factor. For this reason, a mother church should see it as an *absolute requirement* that its role include providing weekly encouragement for the pioneer pastor. This must be done either by the mother church's senior pastor or by an associate staff member with a degree of ministry maturity and senior leadership experience far exceeding that of the new congregation's pastor. For the first year post launch, if proximity to the mother church allows, it may be wise to give young pioneer pastors an office at the mother church and invite them to attend staff meetings there. This, however, should not continue as a permanent arrangement. The apron strings eventually need to be cut.

Coaching and Encouragement

In addition to a supervisory relationship, the leader of a new church will also benefit from the presence of a personal mentor or coach. Stetzer asserts, "A supervisor should focus on work issues and a mentor should focus on personhood issues."[174] Like supervision, but to a lesser degree, frequency of coaching has a significant impact on church plant attendance, with weekly coaching proving far more effective than either monthly or quarterly mentoring meetings.[175]

As I left Westminster Chapel's staff to pioneer Hillside Chapel, the man who had been my direct supervisor agreed to be a mentor for me. Pastor Ward had twenty-nine years of highly successful senior pastor experience and a wonderful way of listening. He knew exactly what questions to ask and how to ask them. Another valuable asset he brought: he had no stake

---

174   Ibid., 94.
175   Ibid.

whatsoever in the success or failure of the project, and he had no involvement or investment in my denominational leadership. This meant that I could ask him anything. I could discuss with him even the stickiest relational leadership issues. I could fearlessly reveal to him my own insecurity and immaturity, something we occasionally need to do to work through to repentance and wisdom. With Ward, I had no fear of political repercussions or organizational backlash. All pastors—church planters or otherwise—will do well to find older, wiser coaches who have no connection to their church or denominational organization. The objectivity this separation provides allows the coach/mentor to play the role of a spiritual director, focusing on the pastor's personal journey and spiritual health, rather than on the new church's numerical success.

Perhaps a newly sent pastor would perceive weekly meetings with both a supervisor and a coach as either a distraction from ministry or a personal indulgence to the detriment of his church. Instead, he or she ought to raise these two relationships to the highest possible personal priority. Mother church leaders must hold the supervisor and the new church pastor accountable to ensure that these essential activities actually happen.

Core Group Members

Perhaps one of the most valuable gifts a mother church can give to the daughter is "the gift that keeps on giving," a core of committed Christian people to serve and give themselves on behalf of the new church. The size of a church-planting core is very important to the success or failure of the infant congregation. An informal 2003 survey by the Foursquare National Church-multiplication Office concluded that core size is a critical factor in church planting success—100 percent of the failed church plants they examined had launched public services with a core of twenty-five or fewer adults.[176] C. Peter Wagner cites research by the Southern Baptist Home Mission Board demonstrating that "churches going public with under fifty have three times the rate of failure as those that start with over fifty."[177] Wagner concludes, "If the long-range plan for the church is to be under 200, the critical mass can be as small as twenty-five or thirty adults. However, if the plan is for the church to grow to over 200 that is too small. The critical mass should be between fifty and one hundred adults."[178]

Malphurs' *Planting Growing Churches for the 21st Century* claims that the size of the parent is not a factor in parenting a church. He concludes that any church of over fifty people "needs to take a step of faith and parent a new church."[179] This statement must be nuanced very carefully. Since a mother church is not the sole source of core group members, it is certainly possible for a very small church to become a mother church. If this is the case, however, a plan for developing and assimilating a core of absolutely no fewer than twenty-five adults must be agreed upon in advance, then adhered to once the project is underway. Most new church development projects begin their planning by setting a date for public launch without considering the question of core size. A better strategy might be to base public launch not on a date, but on the growth of the core. A church planting strategy might make the statement, "We will launch publicly when and only when the size of our committed core group has reached fifty adults."

Frequently, the idea of a core is misunderstood. The core of a new church is not simply a collection of adults willing to attend a Bible study led by the new pastor. The core of a new church

---

176   "Autopsy Report on Failed Church Plants for 2003," (Los Angeles: International Church of the Foursquare Gospel, 2003), 1.
177   Wagner, *Church Planting for a Greater Harvest*, 120.
178   Ibid., 119–120.
179   Malphurs, *Planting Growing Churches for the 21st* Century, 255.

project is a team of individuals who pray, work, and tithe—and who are committed to the evangelistic gospel task of bringing people to Christ through the creation of a new congregation. They are not spectators; they are a volunteer mission squad. They should be led like one. New-church pastors often miss this point. They think their task is to minister to their core as a church. That is part of the task, of course, and the core does need pastoral care. The primary leadership task, however, is to motivate and mobilize the core for missionary effectiveness.

One frequent potential mother church objection to birthing a new church is the impact that a loss of members might have on the mother church. This is a legitimate question, but one that is relatively easily answered. Wagner gives the example of Lake Avenue Congregational Church in Pasadena who sent out sixty people to plant a new church. The next Sunday they introduced a class of new members: sixty-five of them![180] Towns and Porter make the following bold statement: "History has witnessed that mother churches become stronger when they give their members to plant new churches."[181] Anecdotal statements like these, however, need to be examined with caution. If the mother church is a growing, alive congregation, like Lake Avenue was when Wagner wrote the above statement, the loss of new members is often barely noticeable. This, however, is not always the case. Malphurs wisely differentiates between growing, plateaued, and declining churches. Both growing and plateaued churches are likely to benefit from sending out a group of members to establish a new congregation. Growing churches will add to the momentum already present, provide new vacancies for ministry for those who stay, and fill the empty seats with ease. Plateaued churches will benefit from a needed pruning to avoid stagnation and the possibility of accidental pruning.[182] Declining churches, however, should be more cautious before choosing traditional

---

180   Wagner, *Church Planting for a Greater Harvest*, 38.
181   Townes and Porter, *Churches That Multiply*, 19.
182   Malphurs, *Planting Growing Churches for the 21st Century*, 255.

methods of church-multiplication. If a church is nearing the end of its life cycle—the greatest portion of the congregation are over sixty and the church is supported primarily by endowments and foundations—that church might consider cultivating a new congregation within their building targeted toward the new and emerging generations or ethnic populations that are on the rise in the community. Otherwise, a declining congregation is wisest to focus on issues of internal health before taking on a parent-church strategy.[183]

Finance

While it is possible for a church plant to succeed with little or no financial investment from a parent church, "the pattern seems to be that the more money the church is willing to invest coupled with good leadership, the greater the return on that investment."[184] If it is rightly applied, with careful assessment[185] of the parent, the pastor, the plan, and the place with participation in a pre-launch "boot camp" or "church planter's intensive," so that the whole project is executing on the fundamentals of effective church-multiplication, increased funding will very likely lead to greater fruitfulness.[186]

Although more money does not *automatically* result in world-changing church starts; the policies and practices that

183 Ibid., 256.
184 Ibid., 261.
185 Stetzer, *Planting New Churches in a Postmodern Age*, 79. See the chart "Has been assessed?" on this page. Where the presence of a mother church enhances church growth and attendance in the earliest years in the life of a church plant, assessment significantly impacts attendance and church growth beyond the second year. Perhaps this is due to church-planter longevity, which must be enhanced when the founding pastor is well suited for the realities of church planting. "All other factors being equal, assessment assures the selection of better planters with a higher likelihood of success."
186 Stetzer, *An Analysis of the Church Planting Process*, 2–3.

statistically result in more effective projects also cost money. For example:

- Having two full-time ministry staff people at launch results in better longevity for church planters and a very significant increase in average attendance at each year point.[187]
- A big first meeting, which probably translates into an expensive up-front marketing or direct calling effort, significantly increases average attendance at each year point.[188]
- Having the pastor's spouse employed outside the church significantly decreases average attendance.[189]
- Compensating the lead pastor for full-time employment doubles attendance at each year point.[190]
- Emphasizing a strong music ministry, which costs money in terms of additional staff and equipment, significantly increases attendance at each point.[191]
- Strong preaching—which may require luring experienced pastors away from established ministries (an expensive task)—significantly increases attendance.[192]

Jan Hettinga, a prolific parent-church pastor in the Pacific Northwest, reinforces the need for multiple staff church starts and adds to this list the costly benefit of a facility that is available to the plant on a twenty-four/seven basis.[193]

---

187   Ibid., 21–22.
188   Ibid., 8.
189   Ibid.
190   Ibid., 9.
191   Ibid., 14.
192   Ibid.
193   Jan D. Hettinga, "Retooling Transformation: Releasing the Power

In short, the amount of funding received by a new church start is not the determining factor for success or failure—the character, giftedness, and role match of the pioneer pastor receive that designation. If appropriated toward activities that have been shown directly to contribute to church-multiplication growth and success, however, a higher level of funding can catapult a new church past the struggling start-up stage and into the thriving ministry stage. While funding can come from many sources such as denominational support, tithing, extraordinary giving from the core group, or independent fund raising efforts, it is *crucial* that the mother church contribute financially to its new church. This has more to do with morale in the new congregation and in the new pastor—and with a sense of legacy in the parenting congregation—than with the new church's actual fiscal need. The giving of money sends a message that the mother church is willing to prioritize the needs of the new congregation over its own. The amount of support is not as important as the *fact* of support. Gifts should be in keeping with the mother church's size and affluence and the new work's goals and strategies.

Other Contributions

Other benefits a mother church can bring to its offspring range from the intangible such as credibility, legitimization, heritage, theology, connectedness, community, values, vision, prayer,[194] and relationships with other established churches, to the very practical such as leadership, talent, loaned staff, administrative assistance, and help with denominational polity and bureaucracy. Hettinga demonstrates that buy-in beyond that

of God through the Gospel of God." (D.Min. diss., Bakke Graduate University of Ministry, 2006), 169.
194   Wagner, *Church Planting for a Greater Harvest*, 46. "The more deeply I dig beneath the surface of church growth principles, the more thoroughly convinced I become that the real battle is a spiritual battle and that our principle weapon is prayer."

typically present under the church planting metaphor is required for the establishment of strong, vibrant new congregations. The parenting paradigm requires that new congregations:

- Become part of the self-image if a church—"it's just who we are and what we do."
- Become a big burner in the life of the church.
- Become a significant part of the annual budget.[195]
- The senior pastor of the Parent-churchmust *own* the vision for church-multiplication.
- The board of elders and the pastoral staff must *own* the vision of church-multiplication.

As in human parenting, the beginning of a new church must happen in an atmosphere of love and nurture. It rightly occupies significant emotional space in the life of the parent and merits considerable investment of time and resources. This emotional commitment does not end at birth; it continues until the young church has the maturity and strength to thrive independently. In fact, it does not end at all. Resource commitments will decrease over time, but the legacy of having brought a precious, life-giving force into the world will endure for generations. Listen to these words from Ephesians 5:25–29 as they resonate in the context of church-multiplication:

> Christ loved the church and gave himself up for her to make her holy, cleansing her by the washing with water through the word, and to present her to himself as a radiant church, without stain or wrinkle or any other blemish, but holy and blameless ... Feed and care for them, just as Christ does the church.

---

195 Hettinga, "Retooling Transformation," 167.

Mother Church Story—Nurturing the New Church

Background

Dr. Bruce Norquist is founding senior pastor of The Evergreen Church in Burien, Washington, a church of between 150 and 200 people. In Evergreen's earliest days, Dr. Norquist led the way as they stepped out in faith and parented a new congregation to serve and reach the First Nations people in and around Yakima, Washington—on the opposite side of the Cascade Mountains. I interviewed Dr. Norquist in a busy Seattle restaurant in January of 2007.

Interview Excerpts: Dr. Bruce Norquist

The Evergreen Church started in our living room without help from any other church. We were a daughter without a mother. That being our history, we wanted someone else to have a different kind of history, where they were birthed out of a local church. We thought we had to be a certain sustainable size—five or six hundred members—before we launched our first church so we wouldn't be decimated by the hive taking off and leaving us with a lack of workers. As it turned out, the Lord sent us a couple, Jeff and Cindy Yellow Owl, who were called to plant a church on a Native American reservation.

As I found out his intentions, I wanted Jeff—and got him— to be part of my church council so he could have experience running a council. I tried to involve both of them in every area of ministry from children's ministry to preaching—to get as much experience as they could by being part of our church plant. We began looking over in the Yakima area: Wapato, Toppenish. We felt, through prayer … the witness of the Holy Spirit, that this was where he was to start a church. He felt good about it, his wife felt good about it, his kids felt good about it. We had every evidence from the Lord that it was his will to pursue this project: only to find that there was already another church in our denomination some sixteen miles distant from where Jeff and Cindy were anticipating planting their church. The individual who pastored that church was threatened by Jeff coming in, much as people had been threatened by my coming into our area. I wanted to be for Jeff what no one had been for me: an advocate.

We were being resisted at the divisional level. We were being resisted at the district levels. I finally had to come back to the highest levels and, talking to the general supervisor, I said, "It's not like you are doing Jeff or me a favor to allow this. You would be doing yourself a favor. This is an outstanding young leader. This is a church that is going to go. Moreover, he is the caliber of person that could be district supervisor among Native Americans, your spokesperson and ambassador among these people. They require someone from their own race to go back among them and preach the gospel in what would be a cross-cultural situation for us." Finally, having secured the general supervisor's favor on the strength of that argument, we went ahead with the launch.

Within a year, they had grown to about one hundred members, which on a reservation is a pretty good-sized church. They were also able to secure a building, a 6,000-square-foot meeting hall, for about $120,000. We helped them do that. The day they left our church, which at the time wasn't five hundred people, as I had hoped it would be—we were about seventy-five members—we took up a $6,000 offering for them. Then we continued to support them every month, beginning at $500 a month and declining over time to $300 a month for their first five years. We sent work parties. We raised another $5,000 for building materials. I was a little bit jealous that they had their building before we had our building!

To this day, I would say that Jeff is probably on the phone with me at least an hour a week—at least—talking about things that are substantive to the church's growth, and just fellowshipping. Our relationship has changed over the years from being that of a mentor-mentored, to being brothers in the Lord. He has become one of my closest friends in Christ, one of my closest friends ever—of all time. I preach in his church; he preaches in my church.

It has cost us. When we sent him out, it cost us not only the offering and the monthly support check, but they had tithed. Their family had been donating to our church—a small church at the time—something like $1,000 a month, which was a substantial portion of our budget. Plus, they had been workers in every area of the church, both they and their children. It was a real blow to lose them, and a loss of an important emerging personal relationship.

To me, this is the most rewarding thing we have ever done, the most rewarding thing I have ever experienced in ministry. I get off the phone with Jeff and I have a warm glow of satisfaction, as if somehow I am involved in something really significant and really meaningful. It is not unlike talking to one of my children. I get that glow, that feeling as if, "I must have done something right here somehow—or it's the shear grace of God that some good has come out of my life and out of my ministry." I feel that strongly about this church plant. Our church has grown, and so has his. The Evergreen Church has doubled in size since we sent him out. Over the years, we have had work parties and done outreach ministries with them. I think our church feels gratified the same way I do.

I am still holding out for my original vision: five hundred people. When we sent the Yellow Owls out, they went out by themselves, except that they went with our support. I would like to try a project that is launched with at least thirty to fifty people, that has adequate finances to at least partially support the pastor from the get-go, and that has enough workers on board to run a service: a praise team, a children's ministry, enough workers to really run an effective church. We want to be a church that starts churches.

PART THREE:

WHEN

CHAPTER 7
WHAT DOES IT TAKE? A LOOK IN THE MIRROR

Justin is a focused, hardworking youth pastor in his early thirties. He and his wife Aimee began their ministry by taking the youth group at his home church in the Midwest immediately after graduation from the denomination's four-year Bible college. Their profound and immediate success soon led to an invitation for Justin and Aimee to move to a sunny suburb of San Diego to assume the already-booming youth ministry at Southport Christian Fellowship, a fifty-year-old congregation with a beautiful facility and average Sunday attendance of about four hundred.

Southport is made up mostly of first-generation Christians who came to faith in their teens and twenties—many as a result of the powerful evangelistic approach and life-transforming ministry of Southport Christian Fellowship. The people of the church have experienced a good deal of brokenness—and a great deal of healing—and they now find themselves prospering beyond what they dared hope. Their commitment to the church is strong. During his tenure at Southport, Justin had done well ministering to the youth and families and had built good relationships. He and Aimee were well loved. With seven years at Southport behind them, though, Justin and Aimee sensed in their spirits that the time was coming for them to take a next step.

About three years into his ministry at Southport, Justin was growing a bit stale. He decided to keep growing by enrolling in the master of divinity program at a non-denominational seminary across town. His commute to school took him through South Ridge, an edge of town where new houses and condos were being built to accommodate the influx of young professionals who were being hired by the region's booming high-technology sector. As he drove through this community, with its sparkling new sidewalks and clean, crisp, tightly-packed homes about twenty minutes from Southport, he saw the couples out pushing their strollers and driving their Honda Insights and Toyota Scions. Justin began to think ... and then to wonder ... and then to pray ... Perhaps God was calling him to pioneer and pastor a new church here.

Soon Justin and Aimee were in Pastor Roger's office. Roger is senior pastor of Southport. He has served the church for ten years and seen it grow from 150 members to its present attendance. When Roger took over the church, the congregation was financially strapped after five years of declining attendance. Escalating housing prices, which drove the original core congregation to move farther and farther from the church, had catalyzed the decline. Roger's predecessor lacked formal education and was unable to connect well with the newer, more affluent families who were moving into the neighborhood. Soon the financial crisis hit, and Roger was brought in to nurse the church back to health.

In Roger's office, with Aimee by his side, Justin articulated his hunch, "Roger, I have a growing sense—and I think it's from the Holy Spirit—that the best next step for Aimee and me to take would be to start a new church in South Ridge." Roger looked across the table at them. Then he glanced out across the newly paved parking lot at the education wing just now being completed by the construction crews. He noticed the open church bulletin on his desk with attendance and giving numbers just barely large enough to support the mortgage to which they had committed in order to complete this project. *They're ready,* he thought, *but are we?*

After a pause he said, somewhat haltingly, "Justin, it is clear to me that the Lord has been preparing you for something like this. You have been a great blessing to us, and I want to get behind what the Lord is doing in your life. However, I am concerned as to whether Southport is strong enough to support the kind of new church project that would be worthy of your vision. I'd like you to go through the denomination's pioneer pastor assessment program. While you're doing that, I'll get with the church council and see what they think."

Justin and Aimee took Roger's advice and went through the denomination's assessment program. The assessment determined they had the appropriate gifts, personality, and experience to lead the establishment of a new church. Having full confidence in Justin, Pastor Roger still wrestled with the question as to whether Southport was healthy enough—or large enough—to parent a new church effectively in the South Ridge area.

Roger knew that the size and giftedness of the planting core team was directly related to its likelihood of making a significant impact on its target community. Could Southport Christian Fellowship stand to lose that many gifted people? How would it affect the life and health and growth of Southport? He had heard the story of a church in Seattle that had ceased to exist after planting two new churches, and another in Chicago that had wobbled dangerously after planting one. Not only had he heard about them, but one of his church council members had been a member at the church that had gone under!

Another major consideration was the fact that Justin was so loved at the church—and that the church plant would be within easy driving distance for many Southport families. That could result in the new plant having a significant draw on families in both a positive and a negative way. The positive reason for people to go with Justin would be that they cared for him and respected his ministry. The negative reason would be that some people might be bored or disgruntled and could leave in search of greener pastures.

If too many people chose to go with Justin and Aimee, the church could be back where it had been ten years ago—with half the present congregation and half the present tithe! Removing his own ego and ambition from the question was difficult, but Roger could see that, his personal concerns aside, he could not take unwarranted risks with the financial and spiritual well-being of the church over which God had given him stewardship. As he had promised Justin and Aimee, he would bring this to the church council for careful prayer and consideration. But how could they know—really know—if Southport Christian Fellowship was strong enough?

When I first wrote this fictional story of Justin and Roger and Southport Christian Fellowship, it was just that: fictional. There was no Justin, there was no Roger, and there was no Southport Christian Fellowship. Then it became real.

One day, maybe six months later, I had a meeting scheduled with Hillside's youth pastor, Peter, and our Web developer, a friend of his, in a neighboring town about thirty minutes drive from Hillside Chapel. After our Web developer left, Peter looked across the table at me and said, "I think maybe God is leading me to take the members of the Focus 20 Group (read *all* the twentysomethings in the church) and start a new church in Woodinville." Suddenly, my fictional story was not so fictional! My first response was to tell Peter "no." Hillside Chapel was only about three-and-a-half years old and averaging one hundred people on a Sunday. Our budget was too small to allow any significant financial contribution to a new church. Besides, was it wise to cut out a whole generation from the congregation—especially the young adults who are so often the catalyst for growth in a new church like ours? It was too soon and it would be too costly.

I knew, however, that Peter was church-multiplication-leader material. A few years ago, in a desire to make personal connections with other pastors in our denomination, I had joined the Seattle District's Church Planter Assessment Team. Perhaps a little more analytical than the average pastor, I excelled in this role, soon finding myself in charge of church-planter assessment in our district, then being invited to train assessors as part of the National Church-multiplication Team. Because of this involvement, I knew Charles Ridley's thirteen behavioral characteristics[196] almost by heart, and I could see that Peter matched them to a T. Peter was clearly cut out for church-multiplication. I prayed, I consulted with Hillside's Church Council, I talked some more with Peter, and decided to support him—with a few minor adjustments to the original plan.

I tell these two stories because I know that parenting a new church is a scary prospect. How do pastors know if their

196   Charles Ridley, *How to Select Church Planters* (Pasadena, CA: Fuller Evangelistic Association, 1988), 7–11. Many denominations, including Foursquare where I serve, have adapted Ridley's thirteen categories as part of their own church planting assessment process. The characteristics are: Visionizing Capacity; Intrinsically Motivated; Creates Ownership of Ministry; Relates to the Unchurched; Spousal Cooperation; Effectively Builds Relationships; Committed to Church Growth; Responsiveness to the Community; Utilizes Giftedness of Others; Flexible and Adaptable; Builds Group Cohesiveness; Demonstrates Resilience; Exercises Faith.

congregations are strong enough to withstand the stresses of childbirth? Fortunately, a number of indicators can diagnose whether a church has reached its childbearing years. I have identified ten diagnostic signs to determine whether or not a church is ripe to birth a new congregation:

1. Congregational life cycle stage
2. Evangelistic/missional orientation
3. Neighborhood life-stage demographics
4. Youth leadership attitudes
5. Adult congregational age demographics
6. Neighborhood economic profile
7. Distance from church to new residential housing
8. Immigration patterns
9. Average attendance
10. Growth patterns

Congregational Life Cycle Stage

Like human beings, animals, plants, and organizations, churches have life cycles. Some phases of a congregational life cycle are more appropriate to giving birth than others. In twenty-first-century America, we consider the ages of about twenty-two to thirty-eight to be the ideal years for human childbearing. This represents a shift from earlier centuries toward a more advanced age. In the most ideal situation, we imagine a woman finishing high school, beginning college, meeting a wonderful young man in college, marrying him after she graduates, spending a few years in her career, then settling down to have a family. Not many women go through all these rites of passage before they reach twenty-five or twenty-six years of age. Of course, a young woman is biologically able to conceive and bear children at a far earlier age, as early as eleven or twelve years old for some.

At the other end of the scale, when a woman reaches her late thirties—and especially early forties—she begins to worry about her "biological clock" running out. Besides the biological barrier, both women and men in their forties are far less able to flex with the kinds of demands placed on them by the early child-rearing years. A woman's ideal childbearing years make up about 25 percent of her life span and occur in the second quarter of her life. These years are characterized by a combination of energetic vitality and psychological maturity. A younger woman has energy, but not maturity; an older woman has maturity, but not energy. Both are required to raise young children.

Something similar is true of church parenting. The very early stages of a church's life are characterized by energy and zeal. Most often, however, the decision-making structures, time-tested leaders, and financial strength needed to parent are not yet in place. There is also a stage in a church's life when all the energy is gone and all that is left is structure, leaders, and financial strength. The most fertile childbearing years for a church lie between these two stages, which usually comprise 50–80 percent of a typical congregation's life span.

In some nations where Christianity is illegal or persecuted, underground church planting movements exist wherein a Parent-churchmay birth a new congregation after only one year of life. The parenting age in such movements may average only eighteen months. In other models, a church nearing the end of its life cycle may nurture a new congregation as a grandparent might successfully raise a child. Leaders in a more mature church may open the doors to ethnic congregations or may move their own worship service to the early morning, open their building, and provide support as a young minister and a core of twentysomethings launch an 11:00 a.m. service. More churches approaching the end of their congregational life cycle need to give serious consideration to this *in vitro*, or inheritance, model. The model solves two giant problems: the problem of how to provide facilities for emerging congregations and the problem of how to keep existing church buildings from becoming attorney and architect offices instead of worship spaces.

Evangelistic/Missional Orientation

The principle here is: a church that is evangelistically fruitful and mission minded is also likely able to birth new congregations effectively. Because birthing a new church is essentially an evangelistic task, evangelistic passion and effectiveness are required to make it happen. If the mother church lacks passion and effectiveness, so will the new church. The best mother church will be involved missionally on both a local and a world mission scale. Churches that send short-term mission teams into foreign fields and serve the concrete needs of their local communities make especially fruitful parents. A church whose primary participation in mission is sending money to foreign fields may not do as well. That church's best role may to be to send money to pioneer pastors who will launch out of other congregations. The engagement of people in mission and service both globally and locally is an extremely powerful sign of fertility. Social justice churches and congregations whose primary identity resides in their ecumenism may find church parenting difficult as well. This is not said to devalue the powerful societal, intellectual, and spiritual contributions of these churches in any way. However, evangelistic zeal, biblical authority, and clear theological identity drive the development of new congregations much more than mutual tolerance and theological breadth.

Neighborhood Life-Stage Demographics

Who lives in the neighborhoods in which your congregation might consider birthing a new church? Most often, these are the communities on the fringes of the twenty-minute commuting radius around the mother church. As discussed in chapter four, the most fertile neighborhoods for starting new churches are those populated by young couples and emerging families. Another life phase that may hold potential for new churches is early active retirement. Once the teenagers have left to go to college, a couple might relocate to a new community where the development of strong friendships and meaningful life activities become primary motivating needs. These communities may be ripe for new congregations focused specifically on the needs of empty nesters and recent retirees.

Young Leadership Attitudes

Young churches need young leaders—and these young leaders must come from somewhere. Parent-church fertility is strongly related to a congregation's ability to attract, nurture, develop, and empower young leaders. One of the challenges in this regard is that, the older we get, the younger young leaders look to us! The presence of young leaders is a sign of fertility, and a key sign of general church health and potential congregational longevity.

Wise churches undertake an intentional effort to disciple and recruit young leaders and give them significant roles within and over the ministries of the church to ensure the presence of vibrant young faces at church staff meetings and other leadership gatherings. Most denominations have seminaries and Bible schools that train young leaders. These schools typically require students to pursue internships in local churches. To what degree does your church participate in these programs? The congregational health benefit of young enthusiastic leaders is almost immeasurable. Ministry apprenticeships offer an important opportunity for young leader development and empowerment. Parent-church fertility levels rise at a brisk pace when ministry leaders at every level of leadership recruit young apprentice leaders to replace them in ministry.

Adult Congregational Age Demographics

This criterion relates to the average age of adult members of the mother church. The ideal situation in this regard is to have a breadth of ages represented, with a distinct presence of both youth and maturity. Clearly, it is best if the mother church has a sufficient population from emerging generations to form a core and leadership for the new congregation without leaving the mother church barren of youthful influence. A strong presence of people further along in life can provide a stable base of financial support, wise board-level leadership, and counsel for the new church. Again, churches with adult populations in other demographic segments also have options for parenting new churches. Younger congregations can accomplish a great deal on the strength of their zeal, enthusiasm, and momentum and can often find financial resources and consultative guidance from other sources. Groups with older profiles can consider launching new churches with *in vitro* models, or assuming the "rich uncle" role in new churches started by neighboring congregations.

Neighborhood Economic Profile

Church growth often follows neighborhood growth patterns. Pastors in declining, stagnant, or established communities often blame themselves for a lack of growth in their churches. However, church growth often has much less to do with the efforts of the pastor than the pastor imagines. When new people move into neighborhoods, churches grow much more easily, and new churches prosper much more quickly and easily. For this reason, both new emerging communities and neighborhoods undergoing significant demographic shifts serve as excellent targets for the establishment of new churches.

If population is declining in a neighborhood, a new church start will be difficult. If those moving into new neighborhoods already embrace the Christian faith, church growth will prove relatively easy. If the newcomers are not Christians, the fact of their move to a new community may indicate openness to religious transformation. Churches that grow in a new community will be those that feel most like home to the people moving into the neighborhood. When people arrive in a new church they are typically asking the question, "Do I see anyone here that looks like me?" If they do not, they will likely keep looking. For this reason, neighborhood transition and growth does not automatically translate to church growth for every church in the neighborhood. The churches that will grow are the ones that look like the emerging demographic, not like the receding demographic. Assimilating new people across generational and ethnic boundaries can prove to be exceptionally difficult.

Distance from Church to New Residential Housing

New homes are a sign of neighborhood growth. Construction of affordable new homes almost invariably signifies that young couples from emerging generations are moving into the community. Large, affordable residential developments clearly indicate that a neighborhood is fertile ground for new congregational development. In high-technology areas, watch and see who is moving in to these new neighborhoods. If those moving in are educated, upper-middle class, international technology workers, pioneer pastors may find themselves in a situation more akin to global missions, where converts come only after an extended time investment, than to local new church development.

Immigration Patterns

One Monday in the spring of 2006, I took an electronic keyboard to a basement repair shop in the Central District east of downtown Seattle. It was the "National Day of Action," and a series of giant immigration demonstrations had been organized in over seventy large cities by those fighting for immigrant rights in our country.[197] I was forced to park several blocks from the keyboard repairman's house, carrying the heavy, eighty-eight-key, weighted-action instrument through crowds of people arriving for the march. The number of immigrant faces present in Seattle that day flabbergasted me. They formed a one-hundred-foot-wide solid column stretching just shy of two miles from St. Mary's Catholic Church in the Central District to the Henry M. Jackson Federal Building in downtown Seattle. Regardless of how you feel about immigration issues, the undeniable reality is that many of our nation's cities are undergoing a powerful demographic transition. The Hispanic population is growing at a very high rate. We can see this either as a breakdown of immigration enforcement, or as the most powerful church-multiplication opportunity of our time.

Immigrant people tend to be spiritually passionate. I had the privilege to attend a denominational divisional meeting recently. Six or eight white "Anglo" pastors were present as well as two Spanish-speaking pastoral couples and a Korean pastor. The Anglo pastors were complaining of the spiritual malaise of their congregations. Families attended Sunday services only sporadically, and it was like pulling teeth to get people to come to small groups and other midweek events. Everybody was too busy with his or her prosperous American lifestyles. Three pastors, however, were in strong disagreement: the two Spanish pastors and the Korean minister. Pastor Juventino Arredondo

---

197   Lornet Turnbull, "Immigration March, Rally Today," *The Seattle Times*, http://seattletimes.nwsource.com/html/localnews/2002921794_rally10m.html. (accessed September 15, 2007).

reported a packed sanctuary in enthusiastic revival every night of the past week and a congregation passionately desirous of more!

I watched as the Anglo pastors counseled him to be careful of burnout. He replied, "Where the anointing of the Lord is, there is all the energy I need." What about his children? They are as enthusiastic about their faith as he is—involved in ministry and loving it. All of the Spanish congregations in our division are growing and passionately spiritual. The immigration "crisis" offers a fabulous opportunity to start flourishing new churches—especially among Spanish-speaking immigrants.

Average Attendance

We had three vine maples in front of our old house. I say "had" not just because we moved to a new home, but because now there are only two. I pruned them all one summer, and I over-pruned one of them. My former next-door neighbor, who always has a gorgeous, meticulously groomed yard, informed me that most plants can survive only a 20 percent pruning. If more than 20 percent of the tree is cut off, the life of the remaining tree is threatened. I took more than 20 percent off my vine maple, and it was not long before I hauled the dead tree to the yard-waste pile in the forested area at the back of my property. This illustrates the only reason church size is important to the parenting of new churches.

A new church needs a core of at least twenty-five adults and is better served by a core of fifty. If those fifty adults make up more than 20 percent of the mother church, the health of the mother church could be threatened. This applies, of course, only if a "hiving off" model of church-multiplication is employed. It does indicate, however, that a mother church sponsoring this kind of new church project should have adult attendance of at least 125 adults—and that 250 is better. Larger, however, is not always better. If a Parent-church is too large, the new church may not appear to members as part of a significant congregational legacy. Considering both capacity for support and opportunity for legacy, the ideal size for church parenting seems to be about 200–750.

Church Growth Patterns

Looking at all the previous factors demonstrates that church health and church growth are not inextricably related to one another. Even in a healthy church, environmental factors such as disadvantageous neighborhood growth patterns may impede growth. All other factors being equal, however, numerical attendance growth is a sign of church health.[198] It is also a sign of fertility. As discussed in chapter six, growing churches and even plateaued churches likely will experience a boost to their congregational health and attendance when they step out and parent.[199] Churches undergoing numerical decline, however, are wiser to focus on internal issues of church health rather than on parenting new churches.

Conclusion

As a tool to help assess your congregation's readiness to embark upon the crucial journey of parenting new congregations, I have included with this book a church "Pregnancy Test." It is found in Appendix A. I have field tested this survey with real-life potential parent churches and have calibrated it based on the results of that testing. Churches will find that they have both strengths and weaknesses in the ten factors discussed in

---

198   Schwarz, *Natural Church Development*, 14.
199   Malphurs, *Planting Growing Churches for the 21st Century*, 255–256.

this chapter. Do not let a few weaknesses cause you to overlook significant strengths. Combined with prayer, conversation among the church's leaders, and consultation with leaders experienced in birthing new congregations, I hope this tool will help you discern whether your church is pregnant and ready to bring life into the world in the form of a new church. Before you read on, why not take a few minutes now to fill out and score the Pregnancy Test?

Mother Church Story—Are We Pregnant?

Background

Dr. Chris Breuninger is senior pastor of Pine Lake Covenant Church in Sammamish, Washington. Pine Lake Covenant is a stable, healthy, evangelical church with an excellent reputation in its community. At the age of twenty-five, they have just discovered they are pregnant with a new church. I interviewed Dr. Breuninger in his office on the Sammamish Plateau, east of Seattle.

Interview Excerpts: Dr. Chris Breuninger

Interviewer: Tell me the story about how you discovered Pine Lake Covenant Church was pregnant, ready to give birth to another church?

Chris: The church is about twenty-five years old, and the vision was "baked in" that we would give birth to a daughter church. Ever since I have been there, we have been teeing up the question, "When might be the right time?" Every time, we got the sense that, "No, the time isn't right." At one point, it would have been too much staff transition. At another point, we were playing catch-up on infrastructure.

We began studying changing culture—postmodernism and how the church needs to adapt. At the same time, Pastor Tamara [Buchan], our associate in adult ministries, was sensing some stirring in her life. Significant conversations took place involving the leadership team, myself, and Pastor Tamara. In the fall, these three discussions came to a convergent point. She had already undergone assessment. She had already planted a church. We came to the conclusion that this would be a good move—for her and for the church. So we presented the question to the leadership team, "Is Tamara gifted and equipped and called to do this?" They said, "We know her, we think she ought to be doing this, and we think she ought to do it through Pine Lake."

The project is still taking shape: a dispersed church without walls—tiny, missional communities that will gather around affinity or age or passion, for outreach. They will meet in a variety of venues: at Starbucks, at a local pub, in homes. Each community will have its own missional project. Once a month, all these communities will come together for a celebration service. It is a hybrid between a cell church and some aspects of what you see in the emergent settings.

Interviewer: What will Pine Lake bring to this picture as a parent church?

Chris: We're committed to financially supporting the church, along with the Evangelical Covenant, local and national: three income streams. We have money set aside from a church building. We tithed ten percent of the income for a church addition and set it into a fund reserved for a church plant.

The expectation is that Tamara would leave with 10 percent of the people who call Pine Lake home: fifty, sixty, maybe seventy, people. There will be an ongoing relationship, but they are going to have their own constitution and their own leadership. We want it to be a very non-controlling relationship, but we would be in partnership in some aspects of ministry. We want to do "celebrate recovery" as a joint ministry, but it is a new ministry. It is not a preexisting ministry. They'll be doing their own thing, so they're like the teenager going off to college.

Interviewer: In that light, when teenagers go off to college, there is often a certain angst. Are there fears circulating?

Chris: Not widely. I think there are the inevitable dynamics of grief and recognition that there will be loss. Pastor Tamara has been a very good pastor to a lot of people. Some of those people will go with her, but a lot of people who have a really good relationship with Tamara will stay and will miss that relationship.

Interviewer: What manifestations have you seen of excitement and enthusiasm—a building of faith?

Chris: There are a number of things that went before the proposal to plant a church. We had what was called an "Easter Presence," and prior to that a "Christmas Presence," where we cancelled Christmas Eve services and sent out two hundred and fifty people to serve. We did the same thing Easter—two very symbolic, bold moves. We went into convalescent homes, the streets of Seattle, and rehab centers to come alongside people the church often ignores. This was setting the stage to plant this church. I think people are getting the whole missional thing. We laid out experiences to expose people before we started talking about it. Then we started talking about it and people had already got it.

We have been talking about being missional, then we rolled out the vision to plant a church, and some people said, "That's it? That's what it means to be a missional church? They get to have all the fun, while we just do business as usual around here?" We are trying to say, "No, it is one expression, but not the only expression. We're going to continue moving in a missional direction, reaching people that a new church wouldn't reach, while they'll reach people that we are not going to reach."

Interviewer: Is there a launch date?

Chris: By the end of summer, Pastor Tamara will have divested 90 percent of her responsibilities at Pine Lake. Beginning in fall, she will devote her energy to the formation of the nucleus. Around the first of the year we will launch. She'll be gathering a core both from the church and from the community. She's got a notion of what the church is going to look like, but she is operating under the assumption that, once the core gathers, that's the time when shaping takes place.

Interviewer: Will their monthly gatherings have anything to do with Pine Lake?

Chris: It is going to look a lot different than the models you and I are accustomed to: sneak previews, the grand opening, the mailing campaign. That is more modern; this is going to be more postmodern—more organic in nature. With society changing and with generational proclivities so very different, there needs to be a new wineskin.

Interviewer: What about this project of parenting a new church strikes you at a heart level?

Chris: It is what the church has always done, because it is the heart of God. God is a missional God. He sends Jesus who sends us. I spent the first twenty-one years of my life as a non-Christian. I know how good it is to come home, how brilliant and beautiful the light is. It's at the core of what I believe about the incarnation and the nature of the church. From creation forward, it is God who moves out and God who gathers, God who seeks, and God who treasures a people who are away.

I wish I could give you the next chapter of the story. On Sunday we are meeting to vote. We will be presenting to the membership a proposal by the leadership team to affirm Pastor Tamara's call to plant a church out of Pine Lake. If you and I were meeting a week later, I could say, "It was a wonderful meeting, a great sending, a great celebration."

CHAPTER 8
BECOMING A PARENT: A TWINKLE IN MOMMY'S EYE

Before my blonde-haired, blue-eyed beauty of a daughter Natalie Joy was a teenager, she would often ask questions about the time before she was born. She would say, "Daddy, what was it like when I was a twinkle?" This was an important connecting point between the two of us because we were the only two with blue eyes in an otherwise brown-eyed family. She was the twinkle in her Daddy's eye.

Not long ago, however, a big twinkle appeared in her *Mommy's* eye.

Even before Treesa and I were married, we discussed the question of how many children we wanted. Treesa was quick to inform me that she wanted ten—a number I could barely fathom! I was thinking more like three, so my response was, "Let's take them one at a time and we'll know when we are done." Our pretty porcelain dolly Leah Rachelle came first. When she looks at me with her big brown eyes, I feel a little disoriented, as if I am falling into a pool of some dark liquid (not a good thing when it's time for Dad to say "no"). Then came Britton Clay. Passionate, inherently musical, and deeply philosophical—he had blonde ringlets and a million questions. Chief among them was, "Can I go out*soide*?" (Imagine a strong Jersey accent—surprising since we are a five-generation Northwest family). Finally our little joyful twinkle Natalie arrived. Artistic and athletic, Natalie loves to dance. After that came surgery for Dad. We had three children and, with the challenges of ministry and family life, both Treesa and I felt satisfied and blessed. We got a dog.

As satisfied and blessed as we were, God seemed to have something else in mind for us. One night as we were talking before bed, Treesa told me of a dream she'd had the night before—or maybe it was something the Spirit had slipped into her subconscious during waking hours: a picture or impression of a little orphan girl from Africa or South America standing on our back deck, looking in through the sliding glass door. Something in her eyes (dark, disorienting) touched Treesa's heart and sparked—or fanned into flame—what became an unquenchable desire to adopt internationally.

Thus began a dance between the two of us: Treesa venturing out to explore my openness to adoption; me finding a way to dodge her forays by purposefully misunderstanding, by feigning humor, or by subtly changing the subject. This dance lasted a decade or more. Treesa would show me "Saturday's Child" in the *Seattle Times*. I teased her that she thought the videos shown by missionaries when they visited the church were adoption catalogs. One day I came home to find Treesa and Natalie "shopping" for children to adopt on the Internet. They looked at me with puppy-dog eyes and turned up the impassioned vocal soundtrack from one of the adoption sites. I laughed and changed the subject.

Then Britton fell in love. The girl that caught his heart was a beautiful young Sudanese refugee who had been adopted and raised, along with two others, by a family in our church. He wrote an album full of love songs for her, and we got to know her family. It turns out that Britton's infatuation was temporary, but, in the course of this developing friendship, Treesa told this girl's mom of her lifelong sense of calling to international adoption ... and the girl's mom told her social worker at Lutheran Community Services ... and the social worker called Treesa ... and Treesa called me. It was my birthday.

"Guess what I got you for your birthday?" she asked.

I could tell something was up. "I don't know. What did you get me?"

"Five new children."

Though the conversation had a fun, teasing tone to it, I could tell she was serious. There was no dodging or making light this time. She went on to tell me that Lutheran Community Services had told her of a group of five Sudanese orphaned siblings from a refugee camp in the north of Kenya. The camp was closing and they were hoping to find a home that would accept all five of them together. With our other children moving out to go to college, we had empty bedrooms. Could we take them?

I asked Treesa for ten days to pray about it, which happened to correspond to our summer family sailing vacation in the San Juan Islands.

My first reaction was quite selfish. I was looking forward to our not-too-far-off empty nest years, imagining greater personal freedom and a sense of space, a chance to focus on my work without feeling guilty. Though that selfishness took some time to subside, I began to reflect on what I knew about Jesus and the Christian faith. I thought of verses like "Let the little children come unto me." "Greater love has no man than he lay down his life for a friend" came to mind. The whole gospel story and the life of Jesus on what I have come to call "the downward path" ran through my mind. A piece of advice: if you want life to be easy and uneventful, don't pray. Real prayer is a catalyst for adventure. I knew almost immediately that there was no other answer besides "yes," but it took me a while to work up the courage to say it. Finally I told Treesa, "I don't think I could face the Lord or keep calling myself a Christian if I said 'no,' so let's take the next step and see what happens." The months that followed were a flurry, full of foster parent/adoption training, CPR classes, house visits by the social workers, and filling out forms.

As the day of the children's arrival approached, I was in increasing panic. I felt like a great wall was coming at me—like an eighteen-wheel truck roaring down the highway, but as big as a house. I got lost on the way to the airport on the day they came, and then got lost again trying to park! I am sure I have been to that airport over a hundred times in my life, but I couldn't find it that day. The first months involved some significant adjustments, and even now, a year later, we are learning what it means to be a family of … ten … but I realized something the other day. I was driving to a retreat with a mentor and colleague of mine, discussing a potential change of positions at the university. In contrast to the anxiety I felt about the decision I had to make, whenever I would start to tell stories about our African kids, my voice would become animated and my tone enthusiastic. A genuine delight rose all the way up to my heart. That which I had feared most had become one of my life's greatest joys! Right up there with Treesa, Leah, Britton, and Natalie, God had placed a love in my heart for Taban, Kape, Latio, Kaku, and Mariam.

I tell you all this to ask a question: Has God placed a twinkle in your eye?

Parenting a church is much like every other worthwhile endeavor in life. At the same time that it is painful, costly, and inconvenient, it is also deeply rewarding, satisfying, and worthwhile.

Does your church have a twinkle?

I have presented the need for an unparalleled evangelistic harvest among emerging generations and have demonstrated that the intentional birthing and nurturance of thriving new congregations is the most powerful method possible toward the accomplishment of this goal. I have shown that new congregations need more nurture than they have historically received. I have articulated the hope and vision that genuine parental care be invested in every new church project, and that every church will see the parenting of baby churches as a normal, expected, natural part of its congregational life.

If, after having read this work, you perceive that your church has a twinkle in its eye, maybe it's time to take action. As a pastor, I have often asked members of my congregations, "Would you prayerfully consider whether God might be calling you to (fill in the blank)?" The blank might be filled with "serve on the church council," "help plan an outreach," or "play drums on the worship team." Let me use those same words with you: Would you prayerfully consider whether God might be calling you to invest your congregation's resources—time, prayer, money, people—in the birthing and nurturance of a new congregation?

It might be tempting to simply put this book away on a shelf without taking any significant action. I hope, however, that you will genuinely accept my challenge to pray, fully knowing that prayer is dangerous—a catalyst for adventure and a launching point for world-changing spiritual journeys. Live dangerously. Pray. Maybe you'll end up changing the world.

APPENDIX A
PREGNANCY TEST: A CONGREGATIONAL SELF-ASSESSMENT TOOL

1. At what stage of congregational lifecycle is your church? (Choose one. 15 points possible.)

☐ **Infant.** The congregation is just getting started, everything is new, and nearly all efforts are focused inwardly toward self-sustenance. (11 points)

☐ **Adolescent.** There is a great deal of energy. Ideas and enthusiasm abound as the church experiments with new ministries and begins to see the Lord "adding to their numbers daily those who are being saved." (13 points)

☐ **Family Years.** The church has begun to see consistent fruit from ministry efforts, leaders have gained confidence, the congregation has a strong identity, and tested ministry strategies are resulting in significant neighborhood impact. (15 points)

☐ **Empty Nester.** The church has been doing ministry the same way for some time and there may be a sense of "mission accomplished" among leaders. Ministries bear fruit, but there is a prevailing sense of stabilization rather than dynamism, and maturity trumps creativity. (9 points)

☐ **Aging Rester.** The congregation is graying and attendance is declining. The church has a storied past, but the present ministries are losing momentum and there is the sense that the most productive days of the ministry are past. (7 points)

❑ **Life Support.** Attendance has dwindled to a few faithful servants, ministry is supported primarily by endowments and savings, and the primary asset is a facility that is far below capacity on Sunday mornings. (5 points)

2. How would you gauge the evangelistic/missional passion and orientation of your congregation? (Choose one. 15 points possible.)

❑ **Evangelistically Engaged.** Through relationship building and evangelistic events, friends, neighbors, co-workers, and family members of regular attendees are consistently becoming Christians and joining the church fellowship. (15 points)

❑ **World Mission Oriented.** Primary mission emphasis in the church is on sending full-time missionaries and/ or short-term mission teams to do evangelistic work in foreign fields. (11 points)

❑ **Social Justice Oriented.** The church's mission to the world consists primarily or exclusively in serving the poor and/or creating greater opportunities and advancement for disadvantaged or oppressed groups. (7 points)

❑ **Event-Driven Evangelism.** The church stages periodic or seasonal productions designed for evangelistic purposes—and people respond to the gospel in these events—but it difficult to discern whether respondents become active participants in the life and fellowship of the church. (9 points)

❑ **Balanced Missional Priorities.** The church is actively and effectively involved in local and global mission—emphasizing and participating in both evangelism and holistic service to the poor on behalf of Jesus Christ. (13 points)

❑ **In Name Only.** Evangelism is discussed and encouraged from the pulpit, but neither church leaders nor congregation members are effectively involved in reaching the lost with the gospel. (5 points)

3. What is the dominant life-stage demographic of the neighborhood/community your congregation serves? (Choose one. 15 points possible.)

❑ **Singles.** Most rent apartments, condos, or rental homes. (11 points)

❑ **Young Couples.** Many are purchasing their first homes and may be thinking about starting families. (13 points)

❑ **Emerging Families.** Young homeowners are beginning to have kids. Small children are everywhere. (15 points)

❑ **Established Families.** Most established couples live in nicer homes, a little larger to make room for their teenagers. (7 points)

❑ **Active Retirees.** The kids have left the nest and the parents have downsized. Grandchildren may visit on weekends or in the summer. (9 points)

❑ **Seasonal Residents.** There is a population swing between the active season and off-season. This may be a resort or a vacation home community. (5 points)

4. What are the two most prominent adult age demographics of the congregation? (Choose two. 10 points possible.)

- ❑ 18–24 (4 points)

- ❑ 25–34 (5 points)

- ❑ 35–44 (5 points)

- ❑ 45–54 (3 points)

- ❑ 55–64 (2 points)

- ❑ 65 and up (1 point)

5. What are the characteristics of your church and your community regarding young leaders? (Choose all that apply. 15 points possible.)

- ❑ There is an intentional effort to disciple and recruit young leaders and given them significant roles within and over the church's ministries. (3 points)

- ❑ Vibrant young faces are present at church staff meetings and other leadership gatherings. (3 points)

- ❑ The congregation or denomination has an intentional system in place to equip potential young leaders for effective ministry. (2 points)

- ❑ There is a seminary, Bible college, or ministry training institute within thirty miles with a similar doctrinal position to that of your church. (1 point)

- ❑ Your church has at least one catalytic leader, pastor, or director in youth, college, or young adult ministry (or a dynamic associate pastor in another ministry) who has served your congregation for three or more years in an exceptionally creative and fruitful manner. You would hate to lose this person. (4 points)

❑ Leaders of ministries within your church recruit "apprentices"—younger leaders to learn ministry skills by serving alongside them. (1 point).

❑ Leaders purpose to replace themselves by apprenticing young leaders. (1 point)

6. What is the economic profile of the neighborhood and metropolitan area within which your church is located? (Choose one. 10 points possible.)

❑ **Booming.** Your church is located in one of the strongest emerging centers in the nation. Entrepreneurship is everywhere, high-wage jobs are available, people are moving in, and new housing projects are being built. (10 points)

❑ **Expanding.** There is at least one company driving growth. Economic momentum and home values are on the rise, and living-wage jobs are plentiful. (8 points)

❑ **Adjacent.** Your area in an "exurb" or a "bedroom community" economically supported by industries located in a larger city within commuting distance. Construction of affordable new homes and retail shopping centers are signs that new families are settling here. (7 points)

❑ **Stable.** Your area is supported by established manufacturing and older technology industries that provide solid, living-wage jobs, but there are few signs of economic expansion. Housing values are stable, and the only young families choosing to settle here are the children of long-time residents. (6 points)

❑ **Plateaued.** Industries upon which your economy is based are facing competition from overseas and not faring well. Factories are closing, housing values are in decline, and the work force is looking elsewhere for opportunities. (5 points)

❑ **Historic.** There are no signs of economic growth and there have not been for a decade or more. The industries on which the town or city was built are no longer in nationwide demand. Home values have declined and few young families choose to make their lives here. (3 points)

7. How far away from your Sunday location is the nearest new residential housing development of one hundred or more single-family homes? (Choose one. 10 points possible)

❑ Next door (10 points)

❑ Within a twenty-minute drive on a Sunday morning. (8 points)

❑ Within a twenty-minute drive on a Wednesday evening. (6 points)

❑ Over a twenty-minute drive on a Wednesday evening. (4 points)

❑ What new residential development? (3 points)

8. How would you describe immigration patterns relating to your community? (Choose all that apply. 10 points possible.)

❑ A major population shift is taking place as immigrants move into our community. (2 points)

❑ There is a noticeable presence of low-wage immigrant day laborers. (2 points)

- ☐ Educated, high-skill immigrant technology workers and their families are changing the cultural face of the neighborhood. (2 points).

- ☐ There is a visible present of struggling refugee populations. (2 points)

- ☐ Many local businesses are owned and run by entrepreneurial immigrant families. (2 points)

- ☐ It is difficult to see any signs of significant immigration in our community. (0 points)

9. What is your church's average Sunday adult attendance? (Choose one. 15 points possible.

- ☐ 0–99 (2 points)

- ☐ 100–199 (4 points)

- ☐ 200–299 (8 points)

- ☐ 300–499 (13 points)

- ☐ 500–999 (14 points)

- ☐ 1,000 or more (15 points)

10. How would you describe your church's growth patterns over the past two years? (Choose one. 15 points possible.)

- ☐ Rapidly declining (0 points)

- ☐ Moderately declining (7 points)

- ☐ Plateaued (11 points)

- ☐ Moderately increasing (13 points)

- ☐ Growing (14 points)

- ☐ Booming (15 points)

Score Sheet			
Question	Possible Points	Method	Your Score
1) Congregational Life Cycle Stage	15	Choose one	
2) Evangelistic/ Missional Orientation	15	Choose one	
3) Neighborhood Life-Stage Demographic	15	Choose one	
4) Adult Congregational Age Demographics	10	Add all that apply	
5) Young Leadership Attitudes	15	Choose two	
6) Neighborhood Economic Profile	10	Choose one	
7) Distance to New Residential Housing	10	Choose one	
8) Immigration Patterns	10	Add all that apply	
9) Average Attendance	15	Choose one	
10) Growth Patterns	15	Choose one	
Total	**130**	**Add categories 1–10**	

Interpreting the Results

- 100–130: **Ready to burst**: Contact your denomination's church-multiplication office immediately.

- 75–100: **Morning sickness**: You might be pregnant, or it might be something else. Talk to a church-multiplication consultant for further assessment.

- 50–75: **Twinkle in Mommy's eye**: The moment may not be far away. Strengthen your ministries and keep an eye on the thermometer. It might not be long.

- 0–50 **Not now**. It is not time to parent. Invite a consultant to help your focus on crucial issues of church health.

APPENDIX B
PROJECT ONE-FIVE

To reach and disciple generations emerging into adulthood in North America, I propose that the churches and denominations covenant together and agree that every existing church will aspire to birth and parent one new congregation every five years. This goal could be dubbed "Project One-Five" alluding to "one every five years" and to several biblical 1:5s that speak to the need to parent, not just plant, new congregations for emerging generations.

- **Haggai 1:5** (through 9) warns against fixation on projects at home to the neglect of God's greater Kingdompurposes: "Now this is what the Lord Almighty says: 'Give careful thought to your ways. You have planted much, but have harvested little …' 'You expected much, but see, it turned out to be little … Why?' declares the Lord Almighty … each of you is busy with his own house.'"
- **2 Timothy 1:5** reflects the generational nature of spreading the gospel, which is embodied in genuine church parenting and grand parenting: "I am reminded of your sincere faith, which first lived in your grandmother … and in your mother … and, I am persuaded, now lives in you also."
- **Jeremiah 1:5** echoes with the vision and passion of the Creator for new life, a fruit of the nurturance of new baby churches: "Before I formed you in the womb, I knew you, before you were born, I set you apart."

- **Philippians 1:5** comments on the delight of genuine teamwork—an intrinsic aspect of the parenting mode of church reproduction—in the process of spreading the gospel: "[I always pray with *joy*] because of your partnership in the gospel from the first day until now."
- **Titus 1:5** demonstrates that the essential role of a pastoral leader transcends the simple care and feeding of a local flock, extending to the proliferation of new flocks with mature, seasoned leaders of their own: "The reason I left you … was that you might put in order that which was left unfinished and appoint elders in every town."
- **1 Timothy 1:5** resounds with the tone of the parent-church relationship: "The goal of this command is love, which comes from a pure heart and a good conscience and a sincere faith."
- **Romans 1:5** speaks to the scope of our evangelistic call, of which the parenting of new churches is one grace-filled expression: "Through him we received grace and apostleship to call all the gentiles to faith and obedience for his name's sake …"
- **John 1:5** speaks to the growing secular mind-set on our continent and to our confidence that the gospel of Jesus Christ will prevail as we participate with the Holy Spirit in a determined effort to establish new congregations for emerging generations: "The light shines in the darkness and the darkness has not overcome it."
- **1 Thessalonians 1:5** addresses the seriousness and depth of spirit with which we ought to engage in efforts to see the gospel go forth through the birth of new congregations: "Because our gospel came to you not simply with words but also with power, with the Holy Spirit and deep conviction."

Appendix C
Additional Mother Church Stories

Mother Church Story—Sparking
a Parent-Church Movement

Background

Dr. James Hayford serves as senior pastor of Eastside Foursquare Church, a landmark church in Bothell, Washington, with weekly attendance of about three thousand. Over the course of six years, Dr. Hayford has led Eastside to join existing urban Foursquare Churches in the Metro Manila (Philippines) area in the creation of a rapid church parenting movement, which has resulted in the birthing of over one hundred new congregations thus far. I interviewed Dr. Hayford in his office at Eastside Foursquare Church in May of 2007:

Interview Excerpts: Dr. James Hayford

My first invitations to the Philippines were to speak at continuing education classes for pastors. Arriving in Manila, I would be shuttled through the city as quickly as possible. On one of those journeys, I was moved by what I saw outside the window of the car. It troubled me. People are dying. They are in trouble. The Lord planted in my heart a burden for Manila: this very strong thing I had never felt for any place.

Fast-forward about five years. I got an e-mail from Felipe Ferrez, president of Foursquare in the Philippines. He invited me to have a conversation with Foursquare leadership in Metro Manila to discuss how they could do a better job starting churches in the city. They seemed to know how to plant churches in rural settings, but in this city of fourteen million people they had seen a lot of failures. In fifty years, they had managed to plant fifty churches in the city. In the same time, they had planted two thousand in other parts of the country. Felipe asked if I would become an advisor in their efforts in the city.

I had been praying for [Eastside Foursquare] Church, that we could develop a strategic partnership with a gateway city. My idea: "Let's throw our resources into one place where we can see transformation." I knew I would like to see Eastside become a missional church. It came together in my mind: "Concentrate on Manila with Eastside. Help Eastside become a missional church, help the Filipinos with their strategic problem, respond to what the Lord spoke." All this seemed right as I triangulated these three.

I sat down with them and said, "I have ideas, but they would be different than anything you have done before." What they were doing was a traditional approach: send an individual or family to a place, alone and unsupported. Assist them in acquiring a public address system and maybe two months' rent. "Preach your way into this neighborhood. If you can just get loud enough, maybe you can overpower everything else that's going on." If you set up a PA in the provinces, however, you gather a crowd. In the city, people have other things to do.

I was learning from Ray Bakke about holistic ministry. To reach the whole city, reach the whole person with the whole gospel. The whole gospel is a body, mind, and spirit presentation of Jesus Christ. Identify felt needs, address those compassionately and authentically, and it will open up opportunities to address spiritual needs. I said, "This city is rife with suffering. Why don't we address physical needs and see what the Lord would do in the way of spiritual needs?"

What the Lord gave me was to embrace two of their historic values, then add two new paradigms. The historical values were, first, intercessory prayer. They like to pray, but it is indirect prayer. I taught them how to focus their prayers on communities. The second historic value was evangelism. I would say, "See church planting as an evangelistic strategy. It's not a denominational strategy; it is the most effective form of evangelism known to the history of the world." They started casting a vision for lots of people coming to Christ. I got a report this week that, just last month, 384 people came to Christ in the churches we started.

The two new paradigms are, first, community transformation: pastor a community rather than just a church. Serve your community holistically: a community transformation holistic model. The second new paradigm is intentionality. Do this strategically, carefully, accountably, excellently. Part of that was, "We are going to pay you to do this." Eastside Foursquare pays the pastors for three years. We pay teachers' salaries, rent, everything. Each church has a community development project. Half have preschools. We have five hundred children attending our preschools right now, in the slums. Eastside pays one half of tuition; parents pay the other half.

We have had five hundred people from Eastside go to the Philippines. One couple, the Florences, live there, facilitating Eastside's teams. We have another couple getting ready to move. They are going to coordinate construction projects (a lot of the churches are ready to build). Eastside's commitment is about $1.2 million so far, a huge amount of money in the Philippines.

It has affected our church in a very positive way. The church has become more sensitized to the real needs of the real world. For many years, Eastside consumed everything it generated. Our church now gives away thirty percent of its income. We have concentrated almost everything in the Philippines—in giving, in intercessory prayer, in team building, and in going there. There are about two hundred people committed daily to intercessory prayer. This project is one of the major things that needed to be done for this church to get a significant number of people involved in the developing world ... to become a missional church.

We have been able to create an entirely indigenous, rapid church-multiplication movement based on a parent-church concept: eighty-five churches at this moment. We've started one hundred five, but some have failed. Twenty more are opening in July. When the dust clears a year from now, there will probably be one hundred churches. That means we have had an attrition rate just under 20 percent—a little higher than we wanted, but still pretty good. I engaged fifty pastors in the proposition of becoming parent churches. Thirty of them accepted, and, in the last five years, another five have joined. Of twenty new churches at our Church Planter's Intensive in February, half were either granddaughter or great-granddaughter churches. The idea is rapid multiplication. Opening twenty churches in a year, when it took fifty years to get fifty—that's rapid. It has been hard to keep up with sometimes. It has been going six years now from inception, five years in operation. It's a going concern.

Mother Church Story—Surrogate Parenting: The Midwife Model

Background

Father David Rogerson serves as senior pastor of St. Jude Catholic Church in Redmond, Washington, a growing high-technology-oriented suburb east of Seattle. He has provided nurturing leadership during the process through which Holy Innocents Church has emerged as a thriving independent parish ministering to the adjacent city of Duvall, Washington, in the name of Jesus Christ. I interviewed Father Rogerson in his office at St. Jude Catholic Church in February of 2007.

Interview Excerpts: Father David Rogerson

My situation is not so much giving birth to a church; a midwife would be a better analogy. The church of Holy Innocents in Duvall had been established as a mission parish nearly ninety years ago. There was a congregation there that had grown up slowly over the years. Holy Innocents, like other mission parishes, is a stepchild in a sense. They didn't have daily services. They had volunteers who ran religious education programs, helped the needy in their area, gathered for community building, had informal prayer, but then a pastor or someone from a local seminary might come out and help lead a service on Sunday. When it came time for them to build their own church and to become a parish, they got attached to St. Jude here in Redmond because I had been involved in a building project before and because I had some pastoral experience. They had no full-time staff until fairly recently when they got a layperson to help direct day-to-day operations.

In the Catholic Church, we try to look down the road and see where there are pockets of development. Before an area builds up too much, the Church tries to locate property so that, when the day comes, a church can be built. Long-range planning oftentimes helps churches to have a leg up when they are ready to start. Once the parishes are able financially to hold their own, they are sometimes asked to pay back half of the purchase price, without interest, to the Archdiocese. Individual congregations put money into what is called the "archdiocesan parochial revolving fund" that helps new churches get started by making low interest loans available to them. When a new church is started, for the first couple of years, the Archdiocese just runs up a tab with them. It is expected that, when they are more self-sufficient, they will pay back the monies they borrowed when they were getting started.

The various groups from the parochial revolving fund—from the building and planning committee to the Archbishop himself—will sit down from time to time and review the areas of growth and major locations in western Washington where we should be looking at the possibility of building. "Is this the time, or should we be making a note that in five years we should be checking to see what is happening, for instance, on the South Hill of Puyallup?" As things develop, they take the steps necessary to get the ground and to make provisions so that when the church is ready to go it can.

Twenty-five years ago, a pastor had identified some property for Holy Innocents that people were amenable to selling at a very reasonable cost, as an investment to that day when a church would be able to be a full-time parish there.

So when I came into the process, it wasn't as if I was tromping out into the woods and putting a stake in the ground and saying, "It's time to start building Holy Innocents Parish." They already had a building committee together. They had already had a financial drive. What they needed was somebody to say, "We are committed to the project. We will continue to raise funds for it. We will make this work."

Parish status meant that they have their own church life, they have their autonomy, their own identity, their own mission, and they are not looking to another larger church in the area to oversee or to be responsible for them. I am at Holy Innocents one weekend a month. I am in contact with their staff when questions come up. Their lay leadership is really currently their primary pastoral presence on a day-to-day basis. Some of the staff members here try to provide experience, materials, and a sense of what has worked and what hasn't. There is some exchange of resource from the staff here to the lay staff at Holy Innocents. We had a joint confirmation program. Now, Holy Innocents is on its own way completely.

Being a hierarchical church, there are some strengths—and there are some drawbacks. You have a larger organization that can do long-range planning and can make sure there is someone to help. On the other hand, there is always this feeling of "Big Brother." Is the archdiocese going to work with us? We have had our identity. We have had a sense of our mission. Is the priest who is helping out regularly on Sundays going to be willing to work with us and to work within our style of worship and praise? Is he going to pray with us in a way that is meaningful? Is he going to come in and have a strong need to be boss, or he is going to be somebody who believes in collaborative ministry, and will bring his charisms and recognize our charisms?"

How does the congregation in Duvall see me? With the building of a new church, with the size of that community, they should be looking within four or five years to having their own full-time pastor. I am not so much a founding pastor as an interim between mission status and between having their own full-time priest. Some places you see the pictures on the wall of previous pastors. My role will be more like in the baseball journals when there was a strike that year, so there is a little asterisk next to whatever statistics are there. My legacy isn't to be the spirit, charismatic dynamism that gave rise to a parish; mine was a role of more quiet transition between those who had fulfilled that part already and those who would come afterward.

Now that they have a facility that can accommodate the people who want to come and bring worship there, attendance is up by 20 or 25 percent. Having the space and having identity has promoted further growth and further life.

Appendix D
Seattle District Church Parenting Timeline and Checklist

In preparation for the establishment of a new Foursquare church in the Seattle District, the potential new-church pastor will make progress on two timelines simultaneously: a church-multiplication track and a licensing track. The checklist below describes the church-multiplication track in detail and identifies highlights on the licensing track as they apply to the church-multiplication process.

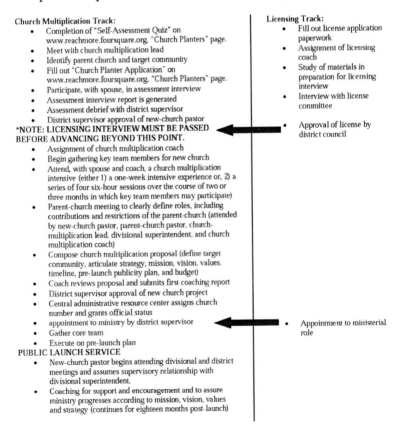

Church Multiplication Track:
- Completion of "Self-Assessment Quiz" on www.reachmore.foursquare.org, "Church Planters" page.
- Meet with church multiplication lead
- Identify parent church and target community
- Fill out "Church Planter Application" on www.reachmore.foursquare.org, "Church Planters" page.
- Participate, with spouse, in assessment interview
- Assessment interview report is generated
- Assessment debrief with district supervisor
- District supervisor approval of new-church pastor

NOTE: LICENSING INTERVIEW MUST BE PASSED BEFORE ADVANCING BEYOND THIS POINT.

- Assignment of church multiplication coach
- Begin gathering key team members for new church
- Attend, with spouse and coach, a church multiplication intensive (either 1) a one-week intensive experience or, 2) a series of four six-hour sessions over the course of two or three months in which key team members may participate)
- Parent-church meeting to clearly define roles, including contributions and restrictions of the parent-church (attended by new-church pastor, parent-church pastor, church-multiplication lead, divisional superintendent, and church multiplication coach)
- Compose church multiplication proposal (define target community, articulate strategy, mission, vision, values, timeline, pre-launch publicity plan, and budget)
- Coach reviews proposal and submits first coaching report
- District supervisor approval of new church project
- Central administrative resource center assigns church number and grants official status
- appointment to ministry by district supervisor
- Gather core team
- Execute on pre-launch plan

PUBLIC LAUNCH SERVICE
- New-church pastor begins attending divisional and district meetings and assumes supervisory relationship with divisional superintendent.
- Coaching for support and encouragement and to assure ministry progresses according to mission, vision, values and strategy (continues for eighteen months post-launch)

Licensing Track:
- Fill out license application paperwork
- Assignment of licensing coach
- Study of materials in preparation for licensing interview
- Interview with license committee

- Approval of license by district council

- Appointment to ministerial role

BIBLIOGRAPHY

Barna, George. "Most Twentysomethings Put Christianity on the Shelf Following Spiritually Active Teen Years." http://www.barna.org/barna-update/article/16-teensnext-gen/147-most-twentysomethings-put-christianity-on-the-shelf-following-spiritually-active-teen-years (accessed March 19, 2010). © Used by permission.

_____. *Revolution*. Wheaton, IL: Tyndale, 2005.

_____. *The State of the Church: 2006*. Ventura, CA: Barna Group, 2006. © Used by permission.

Barnes, Rebecca, and Lindy Lowry. "Special Report: The American Church in Crisis." *Outreach Magazine*, May/June 2006.

Becker, Paul, and Mark Williams. *The Dynamic Daughter Church Planting Handbook*. Edited by Jim Carpenter. Oceanside, CA: Dynamic Daughter Church Planting International, 1999.

Bell, Rob. *Velvet Elvis: Repainting the Christian Faith*. Grand Rapids, MI: Zondervan, 2005.

Biblio.com. "Rick Warren Biography." Biblio.com. http://www.biblio.com/authors/623/Rick_Warren_Biography.html (accessed September 3 2007).

Church-multiplication Associates. "Welcome to Church-multiplication Associates." Church-multiplication Associates. http://www.cmaresources.org/ (accessed November 29, 2006).

Coral Ridge Presbyterian Church. "Children's Ministries." Coral Ridge Presbyterian Church. http://www.crpc. org/2000/Departments/Childrens%20Ministries/ index.html (accessed December 8, 2006).

Costa-Prades, Bernadette. *Little Gorillas*. Milwaukee, WI: Gareth Stevens, 2005.

Covey, Stephen R., A. Roger Merrill, and Rebecca R. Merrill. *First Things First: To Live, to Love, to Learn, to Leave a Legacy*. New York: Simon & Schuster, 1994.

Crompton, Susan, Warren Clark, Anne Milan, and Gilbert Mansour. *Canadian Social Trends 2006*. Ottawa, ON: Statistics Canada, 2006.

Dudley, Carl S., and David A. Roozen. *Faith Communities Today: A Report on Religion in the United States Today*. Hartford, CT: Hartford Seminary, 2001.

Engel, James R. "Using Research Strategically in Urban Ministry." In *Planting and Growing Urban Churches: From Dream to Reality*, ed. Harvie M. Conn, Grand Rapids, MI: Baker, 1997.

Guder, Darrell L., and Lois Barrett. *Missional Church: A Vision for the Sending of the Church in North America*, The Gospel and Our Culture Series. Grand Rapids: William B. Eerdmans, 1998.

Hadaway, C. Kirk. "Learning from Urban Church Research." In *Planting and Growing Urban Churches: From Dream to Reality*, ed. Harvie M. Conn, Grand Rapids, MI: Baker, 1997.

_____. *Is the Episcopal Church Growing (or Declining)?* New York: The Episcopal Church Center, 2005.

Hettinga, Jan D. "Retooling Transformation: Releasing the Power of God through the Gospel of God." D.Min. diss., Bakke Graduate University of Ministry, 2006.

Holzmann, John. "Caleb Project Research Expeditions." In *Planting and Growing Urban Churches: From Dream to Reality*, ed. Harvie M. Conn, Grand Rapids, MI: Baker, 1997. © Used by permission.

International Church of the Foursquare Gospel. "Autopsy Report on Failed Church Plants for 2003." International Church of the Foursquare Gospel. http://supervisor. foursquare.org/images/medialibrary/16___CMI__ complete_.pdf (accessed March 7, 2007).

Jones, Dale E., Sherri Doty, Clifford Grammich, James E. Horsch, Richard Houseal, Mac Lynn, John P. Marcum, Kenneth M. Sanchagrin, and Richard H. Taylor. *Religious Congregations and Membership in the United States 2000*. Nashville, TN: Glenmary Research Center, 2002.

Kaczorowski, Laura. "Willow Creek Community Church." University of Virginia. http://religiousmovements.lib. virginia.edu/nrms/willow.html (accessed September 3, 2007).

Kalman, Bobbie. *The Life Cycle of a Sea Turtle*, The Life Cycle Series. New York: Crabtree, 2002.

Keller, Timothy J., and J. Allen Thompson. *Church Planter Manual*. New York: Redeemer Church Planting Center, 2002. © Used by permission.

Kosmin, Barry A., Egon Mayer, and Ariela Keysar. *American Religious Identification Survey 2001*. New York: City University of New York, 2001.

Lewis, C. S. *The Magician's Nephew*. New York: HarperCollins, 1994. © Used by permission.

Malphurs, Aubrey. *Planting Growing Churches for the 21st Century*. 2d ed. Grand Rapids: Baker, 1998.

McGavran, Donald A. *Understanding Church Growth*. Rev. ed. Grand Rapids, MI: William B. Eerdmans, 1980.

_____., and George G. Hunter, III. *Church Growth Strategies That Work*. Creative Leadership Series, ed. Lyle E. Schaller. Nashville, TN: Abingdon, 1980.

McLaren, Brian D. *A Generous Orthodoxy*. Grand Rapids, MI: Zondervan, 2004.

_____. *A New Kind of Christian: A Tale of Two Friends on a Spiritual Journey*. San Francisco: Jossey-Bass, 2001.

Miller, Donald. *Blue Like Jazz: Nonreligious Thoughts on Christian Spirituality*. Nashville, TN: Thomas Nelson, 2003.

Moore, Ralph. *Starting a New Church: The Church Planter's Guide to Success.* Ventura, CA: Regal, 2002.

Murray, Stuart. *Church Planting: Laying Foundations.* North American ed. Scottdale, PA: Herald Press, 2001. © Used by permission.

Nebel, Thomas P. *Big Dreams in Small Places.* St. Charles, IL: ChurchSmart, 2002.

Neighbour, Ralph W., Jr. "How to Create an Urban Strategy." In *Planting and Growing Urban Churches: From Dream to Reality,* ed. Harvie M. Conn, Grand Rapids, MI: Baker, 1997.

Olson, David T. *The State of the American Church.* PowerPoint Presentation. The American Church, 2004.

Presbyterian Church (USA). "New Church Development: Building the Church One Congregation at a Time." Presbyterian Church (USA). http://www.pcusa.org/newchurch/ (accessed November 29, 2006).

Ridley, Charles. *How to Select Church Planters.* Pasadena, CA: Fuller Evangelistic Association, 1988.

Robinson, B. A. "Christian Meta-Groups, Wings, Families, Denominations, Faith Groups, and Belief Systems." Religious Tolerance. http://www.religioustolerance.org/christ7.htm (accessed December 20, 2006).

_____. "Religious Identification in the U.S." Religious Tolerance. http://www.religioustolerance.org/chr_prac2.htm (accessed April 25, 2006).

Saddleback Church. "The Saddleback Story." Saddleback Church. http://www.saddleback.com/flash/story.asp (accessed September 3, 2007).

Schwarz, Christian A. *Natural Church Development: A Guide to Eight Essential Qualities of Healthy Churches.* 4th ed. St. Charles, IL: ChurchSmart, 2000.

Searcy, Nelson and Kerrick Thomas, *Launch: Starting a New Church from Scratch.* Ventura, CA: Regal Books, 2007.

Sjogren, Steve. *The Perfectly Imperfect Church: Redefining the "Ideal" Church.* Loveland, CO: Group, 2002.

Southwestern Assemblies of God University. "Program in Church Planting and Revitalization Now Offered." Southwestern Assemblies of God University. http://70.86.83.194/news/ article.php?pageNum_ news=10andtotalRows_news =342andID=13 (accessed December 2, 2006).

Stetzer, Edward J. *An Analysis of the Church Planting Process and Other Selected Factors on the Attendance of SBC Church Plants.* Alpharetta, GA: Southern Baptist Convention: North American Mission Board, 2003.

_____. *Planting New Churches in a Postmodern Age.* Nashville, TN: Broadman and Holman, 2003. © Used by permission.

_____. *Planting Missional Churches.* Nashville, TN: Broadman and Holman, 2006.

Sweet, Leonard I. "A New Reformation—Re-Creating
   Worship for a Postmodern World." In *Worship at the Next
   Level*, ed. Tim A. Dearborn, Grand Rapids: Baker, 2004.

Tidsworth, Floyd. *Life Cycle of a New Congregation.*
   Nashville, TN: Broadman Press, 1992.

Towns, Elmer L., and Douglas Porter. *Churches That
   Multiply: A Bible Study on Church Planting.* Kansas City
   MO: Beacon Hill Press, 2003.

Tuckman, Bruce. "Developmental Sequence in Small
   Groups." *Psychological Bulletin* 63 (1965).

Wagner, C. Peter. *Church Planting for a Greater Harvest: A
   Comprehensive Guide.* Ventura, CA: Regal, 1990.

Willow Creek Community Church. "History—Willow Creek
   Community Church." Willow Creek Community Church.
   http://www.willowcreek.org/history.asp. (accessed May
   10, 2007).

Yaconelli, Mike. *Stories of Emergence: Moving From
   Absolute to Authentic.* Grand Rapids, MI: Zondervan,
   2003.

LaVergne, TN USA
29 August 2010
194972LV00002B/9/P